DYNAMICS OF INTERNATIONAL RELATIONS

DYNAMICS OF INTERNATIONAL RELATIONS

MEHDI HERAVI, PH.D.

IBEX Publishers
Bethesda, Maryland

Dynamics of International Relations
by Mehdi Heravi

Copyright © 2005 Mehdi Heravi

Manufactured in the United States of America

The paper used in this book meets the minimum requirements of the
American National Standard for Information Services – Permanence of
Paper for Printed Library Materials, ANSI Z39.48 1984

*Photograph on cover was taken at the Tehran conference in 1943.
The author's family estate was also a host to the Big Three.*

IBEX Publishers, Inc.
Post Office Box 30087
Bethesda, Maryland 20824 USA
Telephone: 301-718-8188
Facsimile: 301-907-8707
www.ibexpublishers.com

Library of Congress Cataloging-in-Publication Data

Heravi, Mehdi,   1940-
Dynamics of international relations / Mehdi Heravi.
p. cm.
Includes bibliographical references and index.
ISBN 1-58814-040-7 (alk. paper)
1. International relations.   I. Title.
JZ1242 .H47 2005
2005047535

Upon completion of this book, the news of mother's passing reached me. God rest her soul in peace.

In loving memory of
R. (B.) H. & A.A.H
K. & E.K.
J.F.P.
All five of them believed that
supreme to all nations is Humanity

to
N
in hope

also this book is dedicated to:
J.S.E.
M.W.S.jr.
P.M.M.
for their kindness, thoughtfulness,
and understanding, but, most of all,
for their true friendship.

TABLE OF CONTENTS

I
PREFACE

This book is written with the hope of clearly presenting dynamics of International Relations, and to provide the reader with a convenient source of essential information. Naturally such a work has inherent limitations. The situation in International Political system is so volatile and changing so rapidly that it is impossible to provide completely up-to-date information.

As is readily evident the scope of the book is fairly wide, particularly in regard to topics of current interest, but in-depth coverage has unavoidably been circumscribed. And while reasonable effort has been made to assure consistency of terminology and uniformity in the transliteration of foreign words, the difficulties encountered in this connection have rendered it impossible to achieve perfection.

I welcome this opportunity to thank my dear friend and University colleague of the past four decades, Dr. Graham S. Kash, the undisputed professor of the English language, who has spent many hours reading the final draft and made numerous valuable corrections. As always I am indebted to him and his wonderful family. During the preparation of this study Dr. Behzad Jalali and Ulrike Eva Schulz gave me indispensable support for which I am deeply grateful. In a variety of ways Bahram Matin, Melody Graves and Sue Ellen Carter were exceedingly helpful. Also, my special gratitude goes to Farhad Shirzad, his help only exceeded by his cheerfulness.

Having lived, received education, and taught in three continents, the author hopes that his background enables him to provide some useful information which as nearly as possible has been stated objectively. Last by no means the least it is sincerely hoped, that this work will be considered in the light of its modest goal and not in terms of what would have made a perfect book.

II

INTRODUCTION
AND OVERVIEW

This work provides an introductory overview to major topics in the field of International Relations. While not comprehensive— no introduction can be—it seeks to orient the scope and major points of contention within the field. These issues and debates form the basis for future further in-depth discussions of world politics.

The discussion begins with a theoretical overview, the "Ideas and Ideologies of International Relations." It presents the major ideas about how the world works: Realism, Liberalism, and Constructivism. It leads off the series because the ideological lens through which one views the world determines, in many ways, what type of world one sees. The ongoing debate among these theoretical approaches continues to define the field and shapes the debates about many other issues addressed in subsequent works.

The investigation next turns to the issues that surround the concept of a nation by addressing "Nationalism and National Unity." The doctrine of nationalism seeks sovereignty for a people, and in the name of the nation, nationalist ideologies have historically produced international violence. The source and reasons for such nationalist behavior are explored.

Within the field, "Power" is the closest thing to a common currency of international relations. Politics, in all its forms, remains a study of social power, and this analysis explores the different manifestations of power in international relations. Depending upon the approach, power can be seen as a material capability, an agenda-setting power, the determining of interest, or the ability to organize and discipline a system.

The series then takes a brief moment for historical reflection, examining the Cold War, the event that came to define the international scene in the second half of the twentieth century. The investigation of "Bipolarization" explores the onset and evolution of the Cold War, its basic rules, and its legacy in international relations. In many ways, the Cold War inspired and produced many of the tools now available to study the world.

While many believed that the Cold War would last forever, it ended rapidly and unexpectedly. Addressing the notion of change in international relations, "The Cold War and After" confronts the complex question of why the Cold War ended as it did and why international relations scholars and practitioners were so surprised by the course of events. The major approaches to the field each tell a different story of this profound systemic change.

Yet, for all the discussion of change in world politics, much remains relatively stable. Addressing the question of "Stability" requires an investigation into the forces that maintain the international system in its present recognizable form. Taken in tandem, these two discussions of change and stability lay out the ever-present dynamics pushing and pulling the evolution of international politics.

Within international politics, perhaps the most fundamental question is "Why War?" The problem of war is unique to world politics, and this analysis explores the range of explanations for the outbreak of violent armed conflict between and among states. Understanding the reasons for war offers a potential path to avoid its future outbreak.

While much of international relations addresses the issue of war, the field has also begun to explore how to end violent conflict. By understanding "Conflict Resolution and the Settlement of Disputes," it becomes possible to see how states and groups can emerge from war and conflict and create a peaceful coexistence. Producing a positive peace is the goal of this normative approach to the study of conflict.

Next, the series will address the everyday practice of states as they conduct the business of world politics through "International Law and Diplomacy." States rely on international law to set the rules of diplomacy and then employ diplomats to follow those rules in pursuit of a state's national goals. International law thus performs an essential function in allowing and regulating the conduct of the everyday diplomacy that produces the substance of world politics.

The series continues by addressing "Colonization and Imperialism." Colonization created a fundamental division in international politics, and the end of colonialism in the middle part of the twentieth century created a multitude of new and independent states burdened with the difficult legacy of colonialism. This experience has shaped the developing world and remains a central reason that it is still developing.

The following investigation explores that gap in development. "International Development" explores the major contending approaches to development in an attempt to explain this longstanding gap between rich and poor nations. For over fifty years, the developed world has engaged in a project to promote growth in poorer nations, with little success. The evolution of development studies reflects the changing relationship between the developed and developing world.

Maintaining global order and facilitating international cooperation on a host of issues, "International Organizations" serve as important institutions in world politics. The most prominent international organization is the United Nations, a critical site where the world comes together to address issues of peace and security as well as human development. As international organizations develop their own personality and agenda in world affairs, they begin to shape the interests of their members. However, many international organizations remain no more than the product of their members' desires.

Finally, this discussion concludes by examining the role that "Globalization" plays in the evolution of international relations. Perhaps the most profound shift in international relations in the recent past has been the forces of globalization. The seeming shrinking of the world through the compression of time and space has produced a truly global environment. Global issues can now affect the entire world at once, just as dispersed groups can act together on a global scale to advance their agenda. The economic and social forces of globalization have created a new social-political space in which international relations occur.

In total, this investigation presents an introduction to the field of international relations. They paint a picture, in broad brush strokes, of both an academic field of study and the world in which we live. They are by no means complete, and, as introductions, are intended to raise more questions than they can possibly answer.

III
IDEAS AND IDEOLOGIES
OF INTERNATIONAL
RELATIONS

INTERNATIONAL RELATIONS

IR—is a broad and ever-expanding field, covering all sorts of social practices that cross borders. This discussion will provide an in-depth introduction to a number of these topics. To begin, though, it is important to lay out the major analytical approaches that have come to define the discipline of international relations. One of the earliest lessons within the discipline was that the way one looks at things, the theoretical lens one employs to analyze phenomena, determines much of what one sees. In his seminal analysis of the Cuban Missile crisis, Allison told the story three times, each through a different theoretical lens. Each lens revealed a different story, a different cause, a different focal point for analysis and discussion (Allison and Zelikow, 1999). The world is a complex place, and it is impossible to understand and discuss it in its totality—any analysis necessarily requires some sort of simplification and abstraction to make sense of things. Theories are one way to do this, each privileging certain things.

For example, a realist looks at China and is concerned about a rising state gaining enough power to challenge the existing balance of power. A realist looks at Europe and wants to keep it weak and minimally unified to preserve existing balances of power. A liberal looks at Europe and sees an expanding capitalist democracy and the further democratization of a unified Europe as an expanding zone of peace and source of global stability. The liberal sees growing capitalism in China as progress toward political liberalization and the peaceful relations among liberal powers. While such caricatures are indeed oversimplified exaggerations of complex theoretical arguments, they belie a fundamental difference in the way different theoretical approaches view and explain world affairs. Three different theories dominate the discipline of international relations today: Realism, Liberalism and Constructivism. Each one will be introduced in turn.

REALISM

Realism stands as IR's original and dominant theory that continues to define the mainstream of the field. Realism claims to examine how the world "really" is, appreciating the real effects of power as the defining currency of international politics. This power-politics approach claims a long and distinguished historical lineage. Early observers like Thucydides chronicled war as a dispute over the balance of power in the international system (1982). Sun Tzu, Hobbes, Machiavelli, and Bismarck all wrote about the importance of power in politics. Taken together, they establish a tradition of the power—maximizing state as the core component of international politics. It is this tradition that makes realism so powerful. It is able to claim that its simple tenets reflect the reality of world politics in the past, present, and into the future. Realism explains how things have always been and how they will continue to be. Realism claims to offer timeless laws of power politics that explain international relations.

Today, realism is based on three spare assumptions. First, realism asserts that states are the relevant actors in world politics. The international system is a system of states, and states alone matter. For realists, the state is the essential element of world politics. The state has an existential existence, beyond any government, king, group, or individual. States have interests that are unique to each state, dictated not by politics or rulers, but by that state's position in international affairs. Realists discount the influence of activists, NGO's, international organizations, multinational corporations, or the media—each is seen as the reflection of a set of state interests, and, when push comes to shove, a state's interests will prevail. International organizations reflect bargains among states, not independent actors. Companies and individuals are ultimately controlled by and work for the benefit of one particular state—nothing is beyond the sovereign control of some state. Most importantly, all states behave rationally. That is to say that states make ends-means calculations of costs and benefits, taking whatever path maximizes benefits and reduces costs. Realists assert that, in the end, it is the rational pursuit of state interests, not the whims of leaders or spirit of populations, which drives state actions in international politics.

Second, realists view the international system as one of anarchy. That means there is no central authority that can bring order to the system. Since all states are sovereign equals, no state can exercise any type of authority over any other state. With no international government, no international hierarchy of ruled and ruler, states are free to do as they please.

Third and finally, realists view power as the ultimate currency of international politics. Power is measured in terms of raw material capability—what force can one state apply to another. Because of anarchy, there is nothing to stop any one state from attacking any other state. All states must therefore fear for their own survival, and ensure their survival at all costs. The only way to do so is to acquire enough power to protect against invasion. Therefore, states seek to maximize their own power position while balancing against the power of others (Waltz, 1979, Mearsheimer, 2001). State leaders therefore respond to the real international environment as determined by the distribution of power capabilities. That distribution of power is the central focus of international politics, for a favorable distribution means protection and influence, while an unfavorable balance of power spells disaster.

This produces the classic security dilemma. With no other way to ensure survival, states will rationally seek power. Others states see this and, rationally, feel threatened by such an agglomeration of power and therefore seek to develop their own counterbalance of power. The first state, seeing the corresponding build-up in the second, then naturally feels a need to further increase its power. And the model spirals onward (Jervis, 1976). States must always be concerned about their power position relative to others.

Whether in the classical form (Morgenthau, 1993), offensive (Mearsheimer, 2001), defensive (Walt, 1987), or neorealist (Waltz, 1979) form all realists share this common framework. The most recent versions of realism, beginning with Waltz's (1979) neorealism, brought the rigor of scientific inquiry to the study of power politics. Neorealism predicts that the structure of international politics is determined by the distribution of power among states and alliances. States always seek to balance against other power centers, guarding against a relative gain by a rival (Grieco, 1990). Today's realism comes in many varieties, but all realists share this same commitment to rational states pursuing power politics in an anarchical international system.

LIBERALISM

Liberalism has long stood as the opposite theoretical tradition to realism. The liberal approach to international politics also claims classical roots, dating back to the works of Locke, Grotius, and Kant. Liberals focus on individual interests and legal structures as the core elements of international politics. Early liberal scholars emphasized the importance of international law, attempting to institute an idealized international legal order in the aftermath of the first world war. The ultimate failure of this "idealism" in the interwar years led to a growth of contemporary realism (Carr, 1939). Whereas realists see all states and decision-makers as the same, rationally responding to external power conditions, liberals view each actor as unique, bringing a unique set of interests, preferences, and procedures to world politics. Rejecting the realpolitik of realism, liberals observe that war is the exception rather than the rule in international affairs, and institutionalized international cooperation occurs far more frequently than realists would predict.

There are many versions of contemporary liberal approaches to international relations. What they share is a focus on individuals, institutions, and the possibility of cooperation among states instead of conflict. Two liberal theories merit a more detailed discussion here. The first is the democratic peace theory. As it sounds, the theory claims that democracies do not fight each other. This is not to claim that democracies are any more or less war-like than other states, but that, over the course of recorded history, there are virtually no instances of two democratic states fighting each other (Russett, 1993). Several near-exceptions exist, each of which can be debated on its merits, but, by and large, democracies don't fight each other.

This theory dates back to Kant's famous essay on Perpetual Peace (Doyle, 1986). Kant said that nations that had republican forms of government, what today would be called a democracy, and engaged in open commerce—free trade—would be able to from a peaceful union that would protect the security of all members (1939). This is a philosophical challenge to realism, for Kant asserts that a democratic community will be safe and secure. States in such a community will not fear for survival, and will not succumb to the pressures of international anarchy. Democracies are able to peacefully coexist absent any of the pressures that realists assert drive inevitable international conflict.

Today, this approach to world politics exerts a powerful push on contemporary foreign policies. States promote free-trade and export democracy in hopes of creating the zone of perpetual peace that Kant spoke of. And yet, liberals are at a loss to explain why the theory works. Some argue that a shared culture of legalistic dispute resolution helps to avoid conflict. Others say that a shared collective identity among democracies keeps the peace. Regardless, the empirical finding remains: democracies don't fight each other.

The second liberal challenge to realism took a more logical path. Neoliberal institutionalists adopt the basic assumptions of realism—rational states in anarchy seeking to maximize security—but assert that states can maximize security returns through cooperation when aided by an institutional structure (Keohane, 1984). Realists had used the prisoner's dilemma model from game theory to show how cooperation fails—states rationally turn on each other achieving sub-optimal results. Liberal institutionalists show that by extending the time horizon by creating a series of interactions—not just a one-shot game—cooperation is indeed the most beneficial strategy (Axelrod, 1984). Institutions promote cooperation by reducing transaction costs and exchanging information, making it easier for states to commit to long-term cooperative policies without the fear of abandonment.

Keohane and Axelrod clearly demonstrate that institutions, both formal and informal, serve to make cooperation possible and beneficial by strengthening reciprocity in an issue area.

The neorealists cannot put forth a plausible explanation for the proliferation of international institutions, nor can they explain the importance achieved by a select few. For example, the level of cooperation achieved in the European Union defies most realist explanations, yet the move toward further integration continues.

Though they do share a common approach and many common assumptions, the neorealists and neoliberals do differ on at least one significant point. Grieco does perhaps the best job of pointing this out. He claims that the major neoliberal challenge is that institutions make cooperation possible in anarchy by reducing the fear of cheating. States are willing to cooperate to realize absolute gains—everyone improves. He counters that realism focuses on relative gains as the major impediments to cooperation. States aren't worried about how much they gain, but are instead concerned about shifts in their power positions relative to other states. (Grieco, 1990). Thus, in a potential situation where cooperation would improve one state's yield from 1 to 2 and a second state's yield from 2 to 3, a neoliberal would assert that cooperation under the auspices of an institution would benefit all and occur. The neorealist would assert the opposite, noting that the second state actually loses is relative superiority to the first state. The debate over relative versus absolute gains as the source of cooperation has become the central point of contention in the neo-neo debate.

In recent years, this debate has become much less of a controversy and much more of an emerging consensus about the structure of international politics. As the two sides engaged each other, they have gradually moved closer together. The consensus has emerged around the anarchic, self-help international system in which states can cooperate under certain conditions. Though often considered so obvious as not to be notable by insiders, a shared epistemological and ontological approach has provided an important base upon which the entire debate could proceed. Since Waltz, all participants in this debate have taken a positivist approach to social science research (Waltz, 1979). All of the participants in this debate speak the same scientific language. This allows them to agree on what constitutes new relevant new knowledge and how to test theories. Because they claim to work in a similar progressive research program, convergence is possible.

Ontologically, the participants adopted a common conception of the international system as the system of states. Again, Waltz began by focusing his theory on this third image; and his neorealist followers, as well as his neoliberal critics, continued to focus their studies on the system of states. Moreover, the states in question are all treated as unitary rational actors. Not only were the participants talking the same language, but they were talking about the same substance.

From this common platform, the neo-neo debate converged even further as its participants adopted many of the same assumptions. Keohane, the leading neoliberal critic of Waltz, quickly adopted the realist assumptions about the international system (Keohane, 1984). In his neorealist rebuttal to the neoliberals, Grieco (1990) points out how the neoliberals have adopted a number of the core realist assumptions and propositions. They all are able to agree on the centrality of states as actors, the anarchic nature of the international system, the principle of self-help, and that relative capabilities are a major security concern for states. Both acknowledge that institutions are worth studying, with the neoliberals treating them as central elements of study and Grieco calling for a realist theory of institutional cooperation. Both agree that cooperation among states is possible. As Grieco points out, "both the realists of the mid 1970's and Keohane in the early 1980's put forward the same empirical characterization of the world."(Grieco, 1990). With so much in common, it is not surprising that many critics see little difference between the two approaches.

CONSTRUCTIVISM

Throughout the height of the realist / liberal debate in the mainstream of the field of international relations, Marxist and Marxist-inspired approaches to international relations emerged as the major alternative. Two events, however, shifted the alternative to mainstream theories to a new ground. First, the end of the cold war, the fall of communism and the apparent ascendance of liberalism discredited Marxist approaches

(Fukuyama, 1992). The end of the cold war also discredited the mainstream theoretical approaches developed to fight it. As the conflict ended, neither theory could give an adequate interpretation of what happened, let alone why. The failure of existing theories to predict and explain such a monumental shift in world politics opened the space for new approaches to emerge. Second, the rise of an epistemological challenge to existing theories gave a new focal point for challengers of mainstream approaches to international relations. Postmodern, feminist, critical, and other theoretical traditions launched a devastating assault on international relations theory. In that, a new approach, constructivism, emerged as the major alternative to realism.

Constructivist approaches to IR share the ontological premise that the structure of international relations is "a social structure... made up of socially knowledgeable and discursively competent social actors who are subject to constraints that are in part material, in part institutional" (Ruggie, 1998). Actors respond not to brute material facts, as a realist might suggest, but instead to the meaning attributed to agents, structures, and practices. Constructivists argue that meaning is produced, not given. Constructivists study this meaning through a focus identity and rules.

Constructivism addresses the "agent-structure problem" ignored by both realist and liberal scholars. Instead of privileging structures over actors, like structural realism, or privileging actors over structures, like game theory, a constructivist approach treats international politics as a set of mutually constituting agents and structures. Structures, as sets of rules and resources, influence state action while the state's practices simultaneously reproduce and transform the international structure. Thus, constructivism allows one to examine the process through which agents create and re-create the international structure of shared understandings—norms (Wendt, 1999). The international system is thus a set of material conditions and socially constructed rules that give meaning to state identities and interests within the system through practice.

Constructivist scholarship has developed a theoretical understanding of how a social structure of international politics is different from a material and rationalist representation. Rather than privileging either agent or structure as analytically prior, constructivism asserts that both mutually constitute each other. Rules and resources shape the structure of the international system. Rules give meaning to resources—the world has meaning only in certain contexts. Constructivists have also explored the power of norms to shape the interests and identities and interests of actors within the international system, offering tangible evidence that "norms matter" (Finnemore, 1996). Moreover, constructivists have made identity and the constitution of agents an important aspect of study.

To bridge the analytic gap between a rule-producing agent and a rule-governed structure, constructivists have focused on social action (sometimes referred to as practice or praxis). The meaning of rule and identity is not an intrinsic quality, but rather an intersubjectively shared understanding continually reasserted through social practice. A favorite analogy is language. Indeed, the analogy is so powerful that many constructivists have "taken the linguistic turn" and use language as the basis for constructivism instead of sociology. Language has a structure that permits expression but constrains the way one may express oneself. Language is created through practice—speech—and is recreated each time people talk to each other. Language has no inherent meaning—the meaning of a world or phrase lies in its use. If people stop communicating, the language dies. As people change the way they communicate, the language (structure) changes. Social action is the site at which agent and structure exist simultaneously to co-constitute each other. Agents, through practice, breathe life into a system. Wendt emphasizes this point: "structure exists, has effects, and evolves only because of… practices. All structure, micro and macro, is instantiated only in process." For constructivists, the "central question becomes how practices at the international level are given meaning within a context of rules" (Wendt, 1999:185).

The constructivist challenge to realism asserts that realism is not "real" at all. Recall that realism posits actors before anarchy, fixed and material national interest before action, and rationality. Social constructivists argue that realism imposes a fixed structure and reality where none should exist. The first critique is that this supposedly objective notion of power and resources and distribution matters. A classic example is that while the UK has a perhaps a hundred nuclear weapons, they are not considered a threat to global security. North Korea, on the other hand, is developing one or two nuclear weapons, and this is considered a major threat to world peace. Why? Identity matters. Material capabilities are not equal—we fear some and not others. If it were the "objective" threat that mattered, European nuclear weapons would be a target of non-proliferation programs and efforts. They are not. It's the identity of the weapons that matters—what they represent.

Rules and identities, fluid and ever-changing, give meaning to the substance of world politics and set the stage for international relations to occur.

CONCLUSION

International relations as a discipline is defined, in many ways, by the theoretical battles to explain the course of world politics. These theories differ significantly, and yet the fundamental arguments presented here recur again and again within the approaches to topical and functional areas. Understanding these approaches allows for the categorization and explanation of the major issues in the field and provides an initial organizing framework for the coming discussion of international relations.

BIBLIOGRAPHY

Allison, Graham and Philip Zelikow. 1999. *Essence of Decision*, 2nd ed. New York: Longman.

Axelrod, Robert 1984. *The Evolution of Cooperation*. New York: Basic Books.

Carr, Edward Hallett. 1939. *The Twenty Years' Crisis, 1919-1939*. New York: St. Martins.

Doyle, Michael. 1986. "Liberalism and World Politics," *The American Political Science Review* 80, December. pp. 1151-70.

Finnemore, Martha. 1996. *National Interests in International Society*. Ithaca: Cornell University Press.

Fukuyama, Francis. 1992. *The End of History and the Last Man*. New York: Free Press.

Grieco, Joseph. 1990. *Cooperation among Nations*. New York: Columbia University Press.

Grotius, Hugo. 1925. *The Law of War and Peace*. Indianapolis: Bobbs-Merrill.

Hobbes, Thomas. 1958. *Leviathan*. New York: McMillan.

Jervis, Robert. 1976. *Perception and Misperception in International Politics*. Princeton: Princeton University Press.

Kant, Immanuel, 1939. *Perpetual Peace*. New York: Columbia University Press.

Keohane, Robert. 1984. *After Hegemony*. Princeton: Princeton University Press.

Mearsheimer, John. 2001. *The Tragedy of Great Power Politics*. New York: Norton.

Oye, Kenneth. 1986. *Cooperation under Anarchy*. Princeton: Princeton University Press.

Waltz, Kenneth. 1979. *Theory of International Politics*. Reading, MA: Addison Wesley, 1979.

Locke, John. 1997. *Political Essays*. Edited by Mark Goldie. Cambridge: Cambridge University Press.

Machiavelli, Niccolo. 1995. *The Prince*. London: JM Dent.

Morgenthau, Hans. 1993. *Politics among Nations, Brief Edition*. New York: McGraw Hill.

Ruggie, John. 1998. "What Makes the World Hang Together? Neo-utilitarianism and the Social Constructivist Challenge," *International Organization* 52:4.

Russett, Bruce. 1993. *Grasping the Democratic Peace*. Princeton: Princeton University Press.

Sun Tzu. 1963. *The Art of War*. New York: Oxford University Press.

Thucydies. 1982. *The Peloponnesian War*. New York, Random House.

Walt, Stephen. 1987. *The Origins of Alliances*. Ithaca: Cornell University Press.

Wendt, Alexander. 1999. *Social Theory of International Politics*. Oxford: Cambridge University Press.

IV
NATIONALISM AND
NATIONAL UNITY

Many of today's international conflicts are undertaken in the name of the nation. Ethnic ties and Nationalism have been blamed for many spates of horrific violence—Yugoslavia, Rwanda, Sri Lanka, and so on. As such, nationalism has become a critical topic in international relations. Understanding the debates surrounding nationalism permits a clearer analysis of the causes and consequences of ethnic and nationalist-based conflict.

It is important to have an understanding of what is meant by "nationalism." As Snyder notes, "One pitfall in using theories of nationalism to understand potential causes of future international conflict is that the term 'nationalism' means different things in different scholarly disciplines" (1993: 183). This point is of particular importance because, in fact, there is no consensus among IR scholars as to the true definition of nationalism. Often, authors interchange terms that are not equivalent or they disagree as to the full definition of a term. "The term 'nationalism or ('hypernationalism') is commonly used, either implicitly or explicitly to mean simultaneously (and confusingly) ethnic national sentiments or beliefs; political rhetoric that appeals to ethnic nationalist sentiments; and violent conflict that is described and justified in terms of ethnicity" (Gagnon, 1994: 131). When using words like "nationalism," "nation," "ethnic," and "ethno-nationalism," it is important to realize that each represents a unique concept. From a methodological standpoint alone, it becomes extremely difficult to test hypotheses and duplicate findings when the hypotheses and the test employ different definitions of the variables.

Comparative politics has amassed a vast body of work concerning nationalism and its related components. Due to the high quality of this work, most international relations scholars borrow their definitions from this body of literature. Thus, before discussing the treatment of definitions in the international relations literature, a brief overview of the comparative politics debate will provide the starting point for the IR discussion.

Nationalism, it is widely agreed, is a modern phenomenon, not occurring until after the 1780's (Hobsbawm, 1992). Gellner's definition of nationalism as the belief that the nation and the state should be congruent is the most widely used and cited (1983). Some works distinguish between state-seeking nationalism, in which a nation seeks to attain its own state (Breuilly, 1993, Smith, 1986; Connor, 1994) and "official nationalism," in which the state seeks to create a national identity for its residents (Anderson, 1991). The important commonality is that nationalism focuses on achieving the merger of the nation and the state. Accepting Gellner's definition, however, begs the question: what is the nation? This question is fiercely debated in the comparative politics literature, and the subsequent failure of the international relations literature to address this debate has become its first major problem.

There are numerous conceptions of the nation. Some say that a nation can be defined by the residents of a given territory, or a collection of citizens (Breuilly, 1993); others believe that a nation is defined by language (Anderson); economic status (Gellner, 1983); ethnicity (Smith, 1986; Connor, 1994); and still others feel that the only adequate definition of a nation is as any sufficiently large group of people who regard themselves as such (Hobsbawm, 1992). Ethnicity, on the other hand, is frequently defined as a group of shared cultural, linguistic, and religious traits, and/or a common myth of origin (Smith, 1986). The important fact to see in this debate is that ethnicity does not necessarily define a nation, and a nation does not necessarily represent one distinct ethnic group. Only when nationalism is defined along ethnic lines can we label it "ethno-nationalism."

There are two key questions that must be asked of all work on nationalism. First, how is the nation defined? If it is defined by something other than ethnicity, then conflicts among ethnic groups are not nationalist conflicts. In a nation such as the Unites States, which defines itself by civic participation, disputes between ethnic groups are not nationalist conflicts. Each group may struggle with the other for position within the nation, but none want to form their own state based solely upon ethnicity. Accordingly, scholars who claim to study this type of "ethnic conflict" are not necessarily studying nationalist conflict. Second, one must ask: how fluid is the definition of the nation? If a nation is defined as primordial, which is to say that an inalienable, intrinsic quality defines a nation, then there is little room to maneuver when discussing conflicts. Two separate nations are therefore destined to remain separate. However, if one accepts the view that nations are merely constructed identities, then it becomes possible to study the instigation and resolution of ethno-national conflicts by examining the construction of the conception of the nation. In the literature, few authors are "primordialists," but the position of the author on this question, to a large degree, influences the type of ideas that may be proposed.

TYPES OF NATIONALIST CONFLICTS TODAY

Nationalist conflict can be divided into three basic categories in international relation. The first is that of a nation seeking a state—so-called small nationalism. Largely inspired by the tragic ethnic violence that erupted in the former Yugoslavia, this category primarily seeks to understand why groups within a state fight. Here, a group of people who identify as a nation are seeking political control over a state and recognition of their sovereignty. Addressing such varied yet related topics as separatist movements, ethnic conflict, and the disintegration of multi-national states, the works discussed here all offer an explanation for the eruption of violence between two or more distinct groups within the confines of a single state. Pan-national unification movements, such as the Pan-Arabism Nasser's Egypt and German unification under Bismarck, would also be considered under the rubric of nations seeking states. These nations exist in several states, but the nationalist movements seek to unite them under one central organization. Given the recent course of events, these types of movements have not been addressed in recent scholarship, and therefore will not be discussed here. Likewise, with the incredible outburst of ethnic and nationalistic conflict, a corresponding thread of inquiry has developed around the question of solving state seeking ethno-national conflicts. This work will be addressed in turn.

F. Stephen Larrabee provided one of the first discussions of the potential links between ethnic disputes, nationalism, and conflict (1990). Writing after the fall of communism in Eastern Europe, but before the disintegration of the Soviet Union, Larrabee discusses the problems associated with the emergence of democracy in Eastern Europe and points out several potential powder kegs in the Balkan region. He correctly predicted "the disintegration of Yugoslavia could prove to be the main threat to regional security in the Balkans—and to the security of Europe as a whole—in the 1990's" (71). Larrabee's main contribution was to point researchers in the direction of the next wave of international conflicts—conflicts over ethnic and nationalistic concerns. Though his purpose was not to offer any generalizations on the links between ethno nationalism and war, Larrabee did serve to identify a fruitful line of research on the links between democratization, economic transition, and ethno-national conflict.

Today, many groups are "discovering" their national roots, and constructing a nationalism to accompany their identity. The rise in the number of nationalities who consider themselves stateless increases the likelihood that one or more of them will resort to war to achieve statehood (Van Evera, 1994). This statement is potentially a reflection of the obvious—an increasing number of people fighting over the same limited amount of land will become increasingly violent—but it reflects an important, deeper point. The continuing rise of nationalist movements is, in and of itself, a potential cause of war. This trend, however, is far from sufficient and quite problematic.

There is no way to identify in advance the saturation point at which the number of stateless national movements causes a war. Nor does this conjecture provide a way to identify which nationalist movements will be involved in a conflict. Fortunately, several more specific approaches have been developed, and we will examine five different approaches in turn.

The treatment of minority groups within a state is one of the most identifiable causes of ethno-national conflict. Quite simply, the more severely nationalities oppress minorities living in their states, the greater the risk of war (Van Evera, 1994). Oppressed minorities may either openly resist or rebel against the state. The most extensive analysis of oppressed minorities has been conducted by Ted Robert Gurr. (Gurr, 1994; Gurr and Harff, 1994). Gurr has compiled an extensive data set of oppressed minorities in his *Minorities at Risk* project, and has developed a model of ethnic mobilization against repressive regimes (Gurr and Harff, 1994). The model examines seven variables: the use of violence by an oppressive government, discrimination, external support, group identity, status of oppressive regime, political environment, and the cohesion between a group and its leaders. Gurr provides clear, quantifiable measurements for each variable. For example, to measure the use of violence by a state, one may count the number of arrests, forced relocations, incidents of torture, or murder by the government. To date, Gurr's model is the most complete of its kind. However, it remains a model of ethnic mobilization, not of violence or nationalism. Though mobilization may increase the likelihood of conflict, it is quite possible that groups, such as the Turks in Germany, may mobilize yet be neither violent nor nationalist. Nevertheless, Gurr's valuable contribution has been somewhat overlooked by many scholars seeking to construct a broader theory of ethnonational conflict.

Oppressed minorities become take on greater significance if they are a diaspora, meaning they have a "homeland," or a state representing their nation. Gurr's variable of external support hints at this quality, but does not specifically identify reasons for support. The decision of the "homeland" to intervene on the oppressed minority's behalf can lead directly to interstate war. Though this aspect of ethno-national war is initiated by a state, and therefore considered in the state led nationalism section below, it is important to note here that the two causes are interrelated—the greater the oppression of the minority, the greater the incentive for intervention.

The initial attempt to apply traditional IR theory to ethnic groups is found in the "security dilemma" approach to ethno-nationalism. First articulated by Barry Posen, the basic argument of this follows the traditional IR security dilemma. In anarchy, two opposing groups fear each other. As one grows in strength, the other will increase its own capabilities, and ultimately, one group will determine that it is advantageous to employ force to end the threat posed by the other group (1993b). Accordingly, stateless nationalisms pose a greater risk of war if they have the strength to plausibly reach for freedom, and the central state has the will to resist the attempt (Van Evera, 1994). As ethno-nationalism grows in power, a security spiral will drive them toward conflict.

The initial and obvious criticism of this approach is that one simply cannot cross apply an IR theory to ethnic groups operating in a domestic setting. Aware of this problem, Posen and others who use his approach only seek to apply the theory in instances where the state has lost its ability to protect groups within the state (Lake and Rothchild, 1996). Posen claims that his method is most effective in the wake of a collapsed regime or empire (1993b). These circumstances create sort of "domestic anarchy."

This explanation, however, does not fully solve the problem of cross-applying an IR theory to an ostensibly domestic situation. Though national groups may fear each other, they still co-exist within a state structure, no matter how weak that state may be. The state, then, contains within its power the ability to mitigate the security dilemma. If the state chooses not to do so, then the state, not the dilemma, becomes the primary cause of the conflict. However, even assuming the rare instance of the complete disintegration of the state leaves a serious problem regarding the unit of analysis. It is difficult to make national groups into unitary rational actors in the same way a realist would view states in the international system. Only in the later phases of a national movement does a representative organization usually emerge to speak and act on behalf of a national group. Prior to the formation of such an organization, the theory depends on some sort of collective consciousness to emerge and motivate the spiraling action. While the degree of intermingling and intermixing of nations may influence the propensity for two groups to conflict (Van Evera, 1994), there is no stated relationship between threat perception and intermingling or intermixing. Furthermore, it is quite often the case that several factions of a national movement may exist and act quite independently of each other. Though Posen feels that his approach assesses local group's strategic views and understanding of group relations, he remains unclear as to the unit of analysis under study. However, his efforts do show that there is value in using IR theories as part of an explanation of ethno-national conflict.

The second type of nationalist conflict is one where nationalist interests hijack the state apparatus toward political ends. Although state-seeking nationalist conflicts have the highest visibility, state-supported nationalist wars can be much more severe. The primary question facing theorists in this subset of literature is: why and how does the nation get the state to fight for its interests? These types of theories focus on how nationalists "hijack" the state and ultimately force the state to pursue and promote nationalism, when it would otherwise not be in the state's interest. As such, the nation ends up leading the state. Admittedly, there is a fine line between nations leading states and states leading nations into a nationalist war, and to a certain extent, the side on which one falls is often determined by one's conception of nationalism. For those who believe that nationalism is a construction of the state (Hobsbawm, 1992), the notion of nationalism hijacking the state is preposterous. Nevertheless, there is an identifiable divide in the literature which permits us to make this distinction. Two areas of analysis will be examined here.

The notion that nationalism and ethnic exclusions are merely the tools of elites looking to secure self interests and consolidate political power is at the heart of this literature. "Violent conflict is provoked by elites in order to create a domestic political context where ethnicity is the only politically relevant identity" (Gagnon, 1994). Quite simply, elites use nationalism as an appeal for power (Snyder, 1993). By altering political power bases to coincide with ethnic exclusions, elites create an environment in which they can advance their interests in the name of protecting the nation while undermining traditional political and economic power bases. Gagnon offers several hypotheses on the extent to which elites are willing to take nationalist appeals. Because power based on an appeal to nationalism is primarily concentrated in a somewhat volatile domestic base, elites will evaluate costs in terms of domestic support and use methods that protect the domestic power base (1994). Thus, nationalist conflict becomes more likely when the costs are outweighed by the popular domestic support for the war.

To ensure that elite actions will be evaluated in nationalist terms, elites create and disseminate powerful myths. Snyder and Ballentine define myths as "assertions that would lose credibility if their claim to a basis in fact or logic were exposed to rigorous, disinterested public evaluation" (1996: 6). The myths are spread through political rhetoric, and become tools to manipulate and mobilize the masses. Myths serve to: legitimize the regime and its goals; mobilize the people to meet the demands of the state; create a scapegoat in times of economic hardship; and battle institutions of free and independent speech which might challenge the myth (Van Evera, 1994). Though elites in any state may employ myths to reach their political goals, democratizing states are particularly vulnerable to mythmaking. Instability in the institution of a free and open media allows the nationalist mythmaker to hijack the public discourse. Since nationalist agitation and propaganda are necessary conditions for mass mobilization along national lines, mythmakers play central roles in the initiation of nationalist conflict (Snyder and Ballentine, 1996).

Often, elite mythmakers lack sufficient power to take control of the state alone. This leads to the formation of various coalitions who will logroll and subsequently employ a myth to further the interest of the coalition. By trading favors, the elites each accomplish their individual goals while diffusing the costs throughout society. The coalition will use the state's propaganda machine to further their interests and perpetuate the nationalist myth (Snyder, 1991).

The most dangerous period for mythmakers is when they suffer what Snyder terms "blowback" (1991). Blowback simply refers to the point in time when the elites start to believe the nationalist myth they initiated. Thus, adherence to the tenets of the myth becomes instrumental for maintaining power. At this point, propaganda increases, dehumanizing others, while glorifying the nation. Elites will use the history created by the myth to rally the people around a cause, thereby claiming historical legitimacy for actions of the state. Most often, this occurs when states are too weak to manage the social challenges presented by modernization. The more elites wrap themselves in nationalism, control the propaganda machines, and face weak opposition, the more nationalist myths will have a role in provoking conflict. War comes to be seen as the only logical path to achieving the goals described in an nationalist myth. Since nationalism has natural allies in the military and military industrial complex, blowback drastically increases the propensity for war.

Moreover, if the nationalist myth does not treat other nations as equally legitimate and calls for their domination or conquest, the likelihood of war rises. When leaders suffer blowback and must therefore fulfill the myth to retain power, these myths that advance some sort of "manifest destiny of national superiority drastically increase the potential for war. (Van Evera, 1994). When nations see themselves as the "legitimate" rulers of global society, there is little to stop them from acting on these myths.

When a nation includes both a state and a diaspora, or members of the nation residing outside of the national homeland, there exists the potential for irredentism. Irredentism is the attempt to redraw boundaries to recover nationals outside the territory of a state and reunify the nation under one state. Not all nationalisms, though, are equally prone to irredentist tendencies. Van Evera identifies three types of nationalisms, with only one posing an irredentist threat. Diaspora-accepting nationalism is content to allow the nation to exist outside of the homeland. Immigrationist nationalisms seek the reunification of the nation through immigration policies. Only the diasporas-annexing nationalisms advocate unifying all members of the nation under one state through conquest or the redrawing of borders. There is an increased likelihood that the state led by a diasporas annexing nationalism may initiate a conflict or war to conquer territory or redraw borders in such a manner as to reclaim the diasporas (Van Evera, 1994).

Irredentism is also closely linked to the repression of minorities within a state, as noted above. If a certain minority is oppressed and consequently resorts to violence, the minority's fellow nationals in nearby states may decide to intervene on behalf of its oppressed co-nationals. The more severe the repression, the more likely intervention (Gurr and Harff, 1994). Such intervention need not begin as full-scale military oppression. It may commence via aid, training, and the provision of arms for a resistance movement. Furthermore, intervention on behalf of threatened minorities may also serve as justification for seeking larger policy goals, such as strategic conquest or the removal of a hostile government.

Because of the growing instances of irredentism, further study in this area is drastically needed. The various types of irredentist action merit further analysis and exploration, as well as a more defined classification. Though not currently present on the world stage, and therefore not receiving as much attention as it should, irredentism has the potential to be the cause of numerous future nationalist wars. Many identify the great numbers of Russians living in the new states of the former Soviet republics as targets for potential Russian irredentism, should a "hyper-nationalist" policy take hold in Moscow (Van Evera, 1994). A better understanding of irredentism is needed to understand the risks of war posed by a state not including the entirety of the nation.

The third and final theoretical category focuses on the use and promotion of nationalism by the state as a tool in policy formulation and legitimation. Unlike the case of the nation leading the state, the state leading the nation involves a conscious decision by the state that a given policy may be better reached using nationalist methods. The key difference is that here, states set policy, and nationalism becomes a method of implementation, while above, nationalism set the policy, and the state determined the method.

Before proceeding, it is important to make the distinction between "nationalism" and "patriotism." Connor offers a useful dichotomy: nationalism is loyalty to the nation, while patriotism is loyalty to the state and its government (1994). The difference is basic, yet profound. Loyalty to an institution is normally not as deep as loyalty to a special group of people. Thus, "the modern state has strong incentives to use nationalist appeals in carrying out its domestic and international tasks. The state's ability to compete in both of these arenas is enhanced by the use of nationalism to rally popular support behind it" (Snyder, 1993: 193). Two broad categories will be discussed here.

The rise of the mass army in the aftermath of the French Revolution put a new burden on the state. To ensure its very survival, the state needed to discover a way to field a well-motivated, effective mass army. Nationalism provided an effective means to this ends. Posen, who has written the most complete work on this subject, claims that nationalism is "purveyed by states for the express purpose of improving their military capabilities" (1993a: 81). True to his realist roots, Posen finds that the pressures from the international system force states to either improve their military capabilities or fall by the wayside. Nationalism increases military effectiveness by increasing the cohesion within the army, motivating the troops to fight, persuading people to "join up," and ensures that troops will still fight even when isolated in the chaos of the battlefield (1993a). For Posen, creating and promoting nationalism is a logical policy choice for a state to make.

Such an argument relies heavily on Tilly's classic assertion that "states make war and war makes states" (1975). The interplay between the requirements for war and the subsequent sentiments created by using a nationalism as a mobilizer greatly influences both the power and make up of the state. While Posen's argument does not offer much explanation on how nationalism causes war, it does illuminate the close and critical relationship between war and nationalism. Because states require support and loyalty from both the army and population for effective military campaigns, a state may decide to inject a nationalist element into a conflict caused by other factors. "Nationalism is as often a consequence of conflict as it is a cause" (121-122). Posen suggests that nationalism may be a necessary condition for any modern, full-scale war.

Because nationalism is so effective at mobilizing popular support, numerous states turn to nationalist appeals so that they may legitimize the regime and its policies. Leaders who find their legitimacy in question or power base eroding often turn to ethnic and national politics secure their hold on power. Though this in and of itself is not a cause of war, leaders who ignite nationalist sentiments often do lead their nations into war. Leaders manipulate the national debates so that their positions are affirmed. The public discourse is radically shifted so that once-radical ideas become mainstream, allowing the leaders to remove challenges to power and secure the backing of their domestic constituency. This may lead to a "diversionary" war justified by nationalist rhetoric. Though hinted at in the diversionary theory of war debates, a formal connection between the two ideas remains to be constructed.

Closely related to diversionary theories are the links between consolidation of power and nationalism. Gurr notes that two-thirds of ethnic conflicts come after a change in power within a state (1994). As new regimes attempt to consolidate their hold on power, they may often turn to war as a means to rally support. New regimes may also employ use ethnic and nationalist rhetoric to make themselves more popular. By framing the war in nationalist terms, the new regime creates a situation in which the population must either support it or remain excluded from the nation. Revolutionary movements often contain an appeal to nationalism, and Walt has demonstrated that states frequently become involved in wars after revolutions (1992). The use of nationalist appeals may exacerbate this trend. Today, the most numerous and intense ethno-political conflicts are in new and quasi-democracies. The fact that elites will often turn to nationalism as a tool through which to gain political power may influence the recent findings that democratization also makes states war-prone (Mansfield and Snyder, 1995). In both revolutions and democratizing states, appeals to nationalist ties may have a strong influence on the fact that both types of state are particularly war-prone.

States also appeal to nationalist leanings to gain legitimacy in the eyes of their people. Many note that contemporary China, in its move toward capitalism, has relied on nationalism to replace communism as the way in which the government legitimizes its rule to the people. States construct a version of nationalism that legitimizes the ruling authority.

THE REVOLUTIONARY NATURE OF NATIONALISM

Nationalism, being the political notion that state and nation must be congruent, seeks the legitimate sovereignty of statehood for a defined group of people. This legitimacy must be conferred upon the nation by those outside the nation—namely other states. Recognition of statehood admits the new nation-state to the "community of nations" and assures the nation that it is a part of the inter*national* system. Regardless of what type and elements of a governing structure a nation may adopt, until other states recognize it as a state, the nation will remain stateless. Taiwan and the Turkish Cypriots, for example, are two nations who have well-developed governments exercising control over territory, but they are not states, in large part, because they lack official recognition as such from the world community. Until a critical mass of states is willing to recognize the independence of Taiwan or the Turkish Cyprus, they will remain non-state entities. Thus, one element of the battle to be won is the battle for recognition in the eyes of the state system. This provides the first important link between nationalism and the international system.

This also gives Nationalism its most revolutionary character, in the international context, because the state system, as it exists today, is a closed system. All the land in the world belongs to some state that exercises sovereign control over that territory. Because the complete nation-state is a spatial concept, it requires an alteration of the existing sovereign boundaries—a shake-up of the state system. Either some land must change from one sovereign domain to another (succession, irredentism) or elements under sovereign control (citizens) must be moved to a different sovereign control (immigration). Either way, nationalism becomes a direct threat to the existing institution of sovereignty in the international context in which it is located.

Such action is revolutionary on two levels. At the societal level, nationalism replaces the existing societal power structure with one that gives pride of place to the nation-state. The nationalist myth overthrows the existing order by shifting power from it to the nation-state. Society is reorganized along national lines. Organizations, institutions, and other social entities that support the nation-state by fostering national identification are strengthened, while those that allow for other forms of identification are either weakened or destroyed.

Nationalism is revolutionary at international level in a contradictory sense. It seeks to alter and preserve the existing order at the same time. Since the advent of the Westphalian state system, the international system has been defined primarily by states that govern a delineated territory. States cannot exist independent of territory, and accordingly, realizing the nationalist myth requires establishment of a new national government in place of an existing governing structure in a given territory. Ultimately, the nationalist revolution will create either a new state or a new identity for an existing state. Nationalism thus seeks to revolutionize the state system by altering its membership and reconstructing the way in which all other states see the system. The complete nation-state is a member of the international state system, and it desires to be recognized as such. The irony comes from the fact that, though altering the content of the existing order, the complete nation-state needs to maintain the state system to become a state. Thus, the revolution at the international level is complex, requiring a change in content but not in the basic ordering principles of the state system.

Indeed, 1989 represented the ultimate triumph of nationalism, for the Soviet Union and its empire, which rested legitimacy not on nationality, but on class, fractured along national lines to the delight of the nations and to the dismay of the commies. Today, nearly all states claim to represent their people as a national state with popular sovereignty. International calls for justice are made on behalf of oppressed people seeking political rights in a state. Nationalism has become in integral part of the modern state system, linking people, through the myth of the nation, to sovereignty, the defining characteristic of the international system.

BIBLIOGRAPHY

Anderson, Benedict. 1991. *Imagined Communities*. Second Edition. New York: Verso.

Breuilly, John. 1993. *Nationalism and the State*. Second Edition. Chicago: University of Chicago Press.

Connor, Walker. 1994 *Ethno nationalism*. Princeton NJ: Princeton University Press.

Gagnon, V. P. 1994. "Ethnic Nationalism and International Conflict," *International Security*. Volume 19, Number 3, Winter 1994/95. pp. 130-166.

Gellner, Ernest. 1983. *Nations and Nationalism*. Ithaca, NY: Cornell University Press.

Gurr, Ted Robert. 1994. "Peoples Against States: Ethno political Conflict and the Changing World System," *International Studies Quarterly*. Volume 38, Number 3, September 1994. pp. 347-377.

Gurr, Ted Robert, and Barbara Harff. 1994. *Ethnic Conflict in World Politics*. Boulder, Co: Westview Press.

Hobsbawm, Eric. 1992 *Nations and Nationalism Since 1780*. Cambridge: Cambridge University Press. Second Edition.

Larrabee, F. Stephen. 1990. "Long Memories and Short Fuses," *International Security*. Volume 15, Number 3, Winter 1990/91. pp. 58-91.

Mansfield, Edward and Jack Snyder. 1995. "Democratization and the Danger of War," *International Security*. Volume 20, Number 1, Summer 1995. pp. 5-38.

Posen, Barry R. 1993a. "Nationalism, the Mass Army, and Military Power," *International Security*. Volume 18, Number 2, Fall 1993. pp. 80-124.

Posen, Barry R. 1993b. "The Security Dilemma and Ethnic Conflict," in Michael Brown, ed. *Ethnic Conflict and International Security*. Princeton: Princeton University Press.

Smith, Anthony D. 1986. *The Ethnic Origins of Nations*. Cambridge, MA: Blackwell.

Snyder, Jack. 1991. *Myths of Empire*. Ithaca, NY: Cornell University Press.

Snyder, Jack. 1993. "The New Nationalism: Realist Interpretations and Beyond," in Richard Rosencrance and Arthur A. Stein, eds. *The Domestic Bases of Grand Strategy*. Ithaca, NY: Cornell University Press.

Snyder, Jack and Karen Ballentine. 1996. "Nationalism and the Marketplace of Ideas," *International Security*. Volume 21, Number 2, Fall 1996. pp. 5-40.

Tilly, Charles ed. 1975. *The Formation of National States in Western Europe*. Princeton: Princeton University Press.

Van Evera, Stephen. 1994. "Hypotheses on Nationalism and War," *International Security*. Volume 18, Number 4, Spring 1994. pp. 5-39.

Walt, Stephen. 1992. "Revolution and War," *World Politics*. Volume 44, April 1992. pp. 321-368.

V
POWER

Power remains one of the most fundamental concepts in International Relations, resting at the heart of most analyses of international politics. Yet power remains a fundamentally contested concept, and each of the different approaches to power motivate different types of analyses of international politics. This discussion will introduce the four major analytical approaches to power and explore how each works in international relations.

WHAT IS POWER?

What is power? Does all power flow from the barrel of a gun? Is money power? Are ideas and information power? One can answer yes to each of these questions and still not have any clearer understanding of power in world politics. All are aspects of power, but different "faces" of power (Lukes, 1974). Ultimately, power is a relational concept, one that has meaning only when expressed as a relationship between and among actors in world politics. This section will reveal the many faces of power, setting the stage for a further discussion of how these aspects of power are present in world politics.

Perhaps the most classic definition of power is Dahl's (1961): Power is the ability of A to get B to do something B would otherwise not have done. Dahl's basic definition posits power as a relationship between two distinct actors, where the first exercises power to cause a change in the conduct of the second actor and therefore the outcomes of this limited social system. It is an almost intuitive conception of power, one that relies on A's capability to affect change in the behavior of others. In some instances, it is easy to see the definition. The stronger A could easily, through the use of physical force, prevent B from occupying a particular space or reaching a particular destination. However, few instances in world politics are so clear-cut. Ultimately, this definition of power rests on knowing what B would have otherwise done and demonstrating that some action of A altered B's progress toward those ends. Again, in many basic cases, it is easy to know, study, and analyze power in this fashion, but many more cases require a more sophisticated view of power.

Bacaratz and Baratz (1962) took issue with Dahl's notion to evaluate power by looking at what B would have otherwise done absent A's use of power. They asked: is it possible that B never had the opportunity to consider a range of alternatives due to A's exercise of power? Their point of reference was the formal committee meeting. The Chair of the meeting set the agenda, dictating what topics would and would not be discussed. Thus, the meeting flowed to the Chair's desired conclusion, regardless of the actions of other actors. In this case, A exercised power, not by getting B to act differently, but by setting the agenda, by limiting the options available to B. A did not so much cause B to act otherwise as A eliminated otherwise from B's range of actions. Given the context, A's power lies in the background, in setting the agenda of a given social situation. This brings a broader understanding of power, one applicable to formal and institutional settings in a way that Dahl's is not. The power to create the rules of a particular institutional setting frames what actors come to see as possible or not, desirable or not. Setting an agenda and writing the rules forms a second face of power.

Critical scholars, reflecting on these two views of power, still saw them as incomplete. Writing from a critical perspective informed by Marxist theories, Stephen Lukes (1974), offered a more "radical" approach to power by offering a third approach to those discussed previously. Lukes noticed how an actor, A, could affect another actor, B, contrary to B's interests. Specifically, could A get B to want to do something that is not in B's best interest. Lukes noticed how workers in a small town dominated by one company refused to organize against the company for better working conditions that would have significantly improved the lives of the workers. The company seemed to have the power to get the workers to want to support the company even when it was in the worker's best interest to protest company practices that endangered the workers.

This third face of power draws on an important distinction— the difference between B's objective and subjective interests. Conceptually, this third face of power involves the construction of interests—A's ability to tell B what B wants. Luke's formulation of this type of power depends on the existence of an externally verifiable and objective set of interests. From a Marxist perspective, these objective interests are determined by the distribution of capital—any social structure that separates a worker from the surplus produced by his labor is against his objective interests. This third face of power as the way in which capital can maintain its control over labor.

These three faces of power all approach power from a cause-effect perspective. Power is the substance, the mechanism, the ability to cause a particular outcome of events. Not all views of power, however, lie in this cause-effect approach to the study of international relations. Building on the work of Foucault (1977, 1980, 1982), many have departed from a conception of power as an object or capability one may possess. Foucault moves toward a relational notion of power. Power is not exercised by an individual; rather, power acts on an individual and makes it possible for that individual to be an actor. Power flows through knowledge and institutions, structuring the order of things. Foucault talks not of power on its own, but of power relations. Power is a relationship between knowledge and action—it creates the realm of the possible. In its essence, power involves a question of governing relationships (1982:220-221). He sees power as something that circulates—like a chain woven through and creating the fabric of society. Importantly, this conception leads to the observation that "power is employed and exercised through a net-like organization" (1980:98). Foucault views "the exercise of power as a way in which certain actions may structure the field of other possible actions" (1982:222).

In relationships of power, power performs a dual function. On the one hand, power makes bodies into social agents and empowers them to act as social beings. Without a power relationship, there can be no social interaction. But in creating bodies as agents, power also seeks to make bodies "docile," meaning that power makes bodies comply with social norms. Power is relational and empowering, for it allows agency in that bodies can use power to act to realize themselves. However, in so doing, bodies are disciplined into a social order. In this respect, individuals become the vehicles of power, not its points of application (1980). Foucault's conception of power examines structural power relationships that create the realm of the possible and thereby constitute the social environment in which actors exist.

Each of these approaches to power shares a view of power as an aspect of a social relationship, one that must be contextually defined. In this case, the particular context is international relations. How do these differing forms of power appear in international relations?

WHAT IS POWER IN IR?

Power is central to any analysis in international relations, but the type of power that is relevant and important depends on the context and the type of analysis. Each of the different major modes of analysis in international relations today relies on a different conception of power.

Realism, the oldest tradition in international politics, has long placed power as the centerpiece of its treatment of politics. Indeed, realism is often referred to as "power politics" because of centrality of power. The classic texts of Thucydides, Sun Tzu, Machiavelli, Hobbes, and others all discuss the use and appreciation of the realities of power. Indeed, to a realist, power is all that matters in world politics—all else flows from the distribution of power within the international system. But what type of power? Realists have long looked to state power, treating state power as force, particularly military force. This type of coercive power follows Dahl's analysis—the ability of State A to get State B to act a certain way. To the realist, in the international realm, the ultimate power is the use and threat of force.

Under a realist and neo-realist mode of analysis, power is treated as a capability (Waltz 1979). In particular, it is the capability of one state to use and apply military force to another state. Power is fungible in as much as one can mobilize state capabilities toward national defense. States must seek strategies to defend themselves from the potential use of force by another state. Thus, the distribution of state power is the primary concern, if not the defining characteristic, of the international system for realists. This is the Balance of Power (Morganthau 1993). An astute realist should be able to predict international outcomes from an accurate assessment of the balance of power.

Yet this view of power in international relations creates a very chaotic, Hobbesian world where power is both the end and means of all politics. Daily experience in international relations shows that this is just not the case. Certainly, when push comes to shove in the most important cases of survival, such a dynamic might in fact be appropriate. In the day-to-day world of interactions among states, however, the use or even the threat of force by state A to get state B to act differently is rare to non-existent. Most international politics rely on other views of power to explain the functioning of world politics.

The neoliberal alternative to realism builds on the second face of power, the ability of institutions and regimes to set the international agenda and govern international interactions in a cooperative or at least non-violent fashion. Neoliberals look to regimes and institutions (Krasner, 1983; Keohane, 1984) to coordinate the daily aspects of international relations. Formal institutions, like the UN, or informal regimes, like international law, rely on commonly shared "rules, norms, and expectations around which actor's expectations converge" (Krasner, 1983). These rules set the agenda for what is and is not on the table within each regime. By limiting each regime to a particular area that it will address from a particular perspective, these neoliberal

HOW DOES POWER WORK IN INTERNATIONAL POLITICS?

The balance of power privileges the large actors in international relations—those with military force. An even balance of power provides stability, and states have two options to balance against an external power (Waltz, 1979). First, states might seek alliances (Snyder and Diesing, 1977). Grouping states together against a common foe aggrandizes power, creating a stable balance. If allies are unavailable or undesirable, the second balancing mechanism available to states is "internal balancing," which is an improvement of a state's military capability. Thus, a state might build a bigger army or navy. In the pre-World War I period, states routinely shifted alliances to preserve the balance of power. The post-war development of the bi-polar cold war presented an interesting dilemma: the superpowers were so strong and powerful that adding and subtracting allies had only a minimal effect on the overall balance of power. As a result, the superpowers relied on an internal balancing strategy driven by nuclear weaponry and intercontinental delivery systems to maintain equilibrium (Sagan and Waltz, 1995). Nuclear weapons present the ultimate opportunity for a state to increase its security and recast the balance of power without relying on allies. Where you have the possibility of a nuclear exchange—the US / USSR or India / Pakistan—it comes to dominate the discussion of security relations.

Nuclear weapons are, perhaps, the ultimate form of power a state can acquire. The sheer destructive force of nuclear weapons, especially when coupled with a long-range missile delivery system, allows a state to compensate for otherwise diminished capabilities. For example, Pakistan, a state with substantially fewer internal capabilities than India, has used its nuclear program to equalize its standing vis-à-vis India in their regional struggle. It is no accident that today's "rogue" states all seek nuclear weapons—it's the logical realist strategy for an otherwise weak state to balance the overwhelming capability of the United States.

The end of the cold war destroyed one superpower but left the other standing tall. Today the United States occupies the role of global hegemon in a unipolar international system (Gilpin, 1981, Krauthammer, 1990/91). The gap in material state capabilities between the United States and its nearest competitor is vast—perhaps wider than at any point in modern history. The ability of the United States to use apply lethal military force to any point on the globe with relative ease is unmatched even by its closest NATO allies. The Hegemonic United States is, in many respects, a modern hyperpower.

While the US conventional military capability far outclasses the rest of the world, the global balance of power has not changed all that much since the end of the cold war in the realm of nuclear weapons (Waltz 1993). The US and Russia still retain their nuclear arsenals and cold war strategy of deterrence. If anything, the balance of power has become more diffuse as new nuclear weapons states have emerged—India, Pakistan, Israel and North Korea—also other states are actively seeking to develop nuclear weapons. Indeed, it becomes easy to see, from this analysis, why the realist thinkers in the current US administration so fear the proliferation of weapons of mass destruction. With nuclear weapons serving as the great equalizer, the ultimate potential power in international politics, any increase in the number of nuclear states necessarily dilutes US power and international standing. It is relatively easy for the US to establish and maintain an international order based on its predominant power position in the world, but it becomes equally easy for any nuclear capable state to opt out of that order without fear of reprisal. In a realist world, the ability to deliver a nuclear weapon allows a small state to act like a big one.

The liberal, second face of power also has an important role in international relations. International institutions set a particular agenda for world politics. A skillful actor can manipulate this agenda to direct the course of events with little regard to size or capability. Moreover, states that do not invest in material capabilities can nonetheless play a major role in world politics by adjusting the international agenda.

An interesting case in point is how the French and British ultimately brought the US into Bosnia. After the failure of the UN mission, France and Britain threatened to pull their forces out of Bosnia, and in so doing, activate a NATO contingency plan that would require US participation in the withdrawal. The US was then stuck—it could either intervene in a retreat or intervene to protect its allies and solve the crisis, which is ultimately what happened.

The power of institutions in world politics to shape international outcomes is significant. As noted above, the vast majority of international issues are not the "high politics" that revolve around the distribution of material capabilities. These daily yet important issues, like trade, travel, migration, finance, law enforcement, human rights, and so on, are managed through well established and well respected international institutions. These institutions are a source and site of power for those struggling to set the international agenda with respect to these issues. AIDS, long an important global health issue, became a global security threat of immense proportions once the UN Security Council held a special session on the disease and created a fund to combat its spread. The toll of AIDS was no less threatening to world security before these actions, but prior to being raised in the Security Council, AIDS remained a second-tier global health issue. Only after it was placed on the international agenda did it get the attention that it now receives. AIDS' spot on the international agenda was a power struggle between those who wanted to focus on other diseases and those who viewed the threat from AIDS as especially unique and catastrophic. The outcome of that power struggle shapes the lives of millions.

Globalization has given new life to those who study the power of international capital to reshape the interests of significant portions of society. With the globalization of political economy, in many respects, global capital has been able to liberate itself from the state and become an international actor in its own right. Global financiers have demonstrated their ability to crash international currencies and sway international markets. The prescription for avoiding such a situation, the so-called "Washington Consensus," lists a host of IMF prescribed actions, including reducing budget deficit, taming inflation, raising taxes, and opening currency and trade markets to international competition. These policies, while good for capital seeking a high return, are frequently disastrous for the states who adopt them. Nonetheless, many states feel compelled to follow the Consensus despite its damaging effects.

Another consequence of globalization has been the rise in international networks of policy entrepreneurs who seek to change world politics. These entrepreneurs, such as the global coalition to ban landmines, have tapped into the power of networks, ideas, and language to shape the environment of possible. Individuals and states alike have come to understand the power of language, meaning, identities, and norms as important and powerful elements of world politics.

Of particular note is the rise of identity politics as a salient factor in international relations. The struggle to define and redefine a particular identity is a powerful move because identity claims are a critical power in international relations. Slobodon Milosevic was able to dismantle Yugoslav identity and create a nationalist Serbian identity as the salient political force among the people in the former Yugoslavia with deadly consequences. Hamas has added political Islam to the core components of Palestinian identity. In both cases, the ideas about what it means to be a member of a particular group create the conditions under which some members are able to manipulate their members to kill on behalf of that identity. A communist Yugoslavia avoided deadly inter-ethnic violence. Secular Palestinian nationalism did not produce suicide bombers. Recasting these identities changed the way people fought for them.

This language of identity creates legitimate and acceptable behavior. The power of language is the power of the possible. This more sophisticated view of power within world politics appreciates the fact that tanks don't drive themselves. The material elements of state power are useless without people to produce and operate them. The legitimacy of a government is not a material or even an institutional factor—it is a complex power play resting on language and ideas, social bonds that bind a network of people together. This is not the power to cause, but the power to allow, channel, and create. It is a power not limited to states, it is a power relationship open to all. NGOs can ban landmines. Individuals can launch a clash of civilizations. States can reshape societies and cultures.

The power of identity, legitimacy, and language shapes the cultures in which individuals live. It is here that the true face of American hegemony is revealed—not only does the US possess the greatest military force in the world, but it also projects a powerful language and culture—an open, expressive, tolerant, capitalist, opportunistic, star-driven, action-packed, set of values that shape the wants, desires, interests and identities of people worldwide. Children worldwide now want to dress like Britney Spears, play sports like Michael Jordan, and be as rich as Bill Gates and have a personal web-site. Yet, the mechanisms that transmit all of these American cultural, corporate, and governmental ideas don't belong exclusively to the US government or American businesses. Anyone who can master the right skills of persuasive and compelling communication and show people how to look at the world in a new and different way can employ and use this same kind of power. Anyone can use this power, if only they are willing to play within the US dominated capitalist cultural system that creates it.

Power is a central concept to international relations, but it is not one with an easy definition or treatment. Power is not a thing or a goal or such in and of itself; it's a relationship, a means, a flow that must be put to use. One can explain how power works, but only within a given context, within a given relationship. The real question is not what is power, but rather, the question is who is using what type of power to what ends.

BIBLIOGRAPHY

Bachrach and Baratz. 1962. "The Two Faces of Power," *The American Political Science Review* 56. pp. 947-52.

Cox, Robert. 1987. *Production, Power, and World Order*. New York: Columbia University Press.

Dahl, Robert. 1961. *Who Governs? Democracy and Power in an American City*. New Haven: Yale University Press.

Foucault. Michelle. 1977. *Discipline and Punish*. New York: Pantheon Books.

Foucault. Michelle. 1980. *Power / Knowledge*. New York: Pantheon Books

Foucault. Michelle. 1982. "The Subject and Power," Afterword in Dreyfus and Rabinow, *Michele Foucault: Beyond Structuralism and Hermeneutics*. Chicago: The University of Chicago Press. Pages 208-226.

Gilpin, Robert. 1981. *War and Change in World Politics*. Cambridge: Cambridge University Press.

Guzzini, Stefano. 1993. "Structural Power," *International Organization* 47, Summer. pp. 443-78.

Keohane, Robert. 1984. *After Hegemony*. Princeton: Princeton University Press.

Krasner, Stephen. 1983. *International Regimes*. Ithaca: Cornell University Press.

Krauthammer, Charles. 1990/91. "The Unipolar Moment," *Foreign Affairs: America and the World 1990/91* 70:1. pp. 23-33.

Lukes, Steven. 1974. *Power: A Radical View*. New York: MacMillan.

Morgenthau, Hans. 1993. *Politics Among Nations*, Brief Edition. New York: McGraw Hill.

Nye, Joseph. 1990. *Bound to Lead*. New York, Basic Books.

Sagan, Scott and Kennet Waltz. 1995. *The Spread of Nuclear Weapons*: A Debate. New York: W.W. Norton.

Snyder, Glenn and Paul Diesing. 1977. *Conflict Among Nations*. Princeton: Princeton University Press.

Wallerstein, Immanuel. 1974. *The Modern World-System*. New York: Academic Press

Waltz, Kenneth. 1993. "The Emerging Structure of International Politics," *International Security* 18:2, Fall. pp. 44-79.

Waltz, Kenneth. 1979. *Theory of International Politics*. Reading, MA: Addison Wesley.

Wendt, Alexander. 1999. *Social Theory of International Politics*. Oxford: Cambridge University Press.

VI

BIPOLARIZATION

The history of the twentieth century was dominated by the Cold War, the global superpower struggle between the United States and the Soviet Union. The cold war led to a bipolarization of world politics. With hindsight, it's much easier to assess the dynamics that led to the bipolarization of world politics and a 45 year deep-freeze on many parts of the global agenda. However, it is important to appreciate the difficulties and dilemmas faced by a war-weary alliance in 1945. No one could foresee the depth, rigidity, and seemingly intractable nature of the cold war in its early days, just as no one could anticipate its sudden end in its waning moments.

BEGINNING OF THE COLD WAR

The beginning of a bipolar world order can be traced to the end of World War II, which was the end of a short-lived system of tri-polarity (Schweller, 1998). Late in the war, the deep thinkers among the Allied long-term planning staffs realized that they would probably win the war and would have a twice-in-a-lifetime chance to shape the peace. Having seen the post-WWI settlement fail miserably, they were determined to avoid the pitfalls of the League of Nations and closed international economic order that led to the war. The "Big Three" allies—the US, UK, and USSR—had several conferences to discuss the end of the war and develop post-war plans at the Tehran, Yalta and Potsdam conferences. Here, the US and USSR came to terms with the fact that each would control the areas it had liberated from Germany, the defeated third pole. As the war drew to a close and the Allied armies met in Central Europe, the allies had to decide what to do with the liberated territory. The US was interested in promoting its Atlantic Charter goals—democracy and open markets. The war had pulled it from the depths of depression and had awakened a mammoth military, industrial, and technological base, unrivaled in the world. The UK was concerned with protecting what was left of its colonial empire in a last-ditch attempt to salvage their deteriorating position as a great power. Yet the cost of empire was too great and the UK was devastated by the war, and Britain slipped from global to great power. The Soviets were concerned with establishing a security zone around themselves to prevent another invasion, and had used the war to mobilize a massive industrial and military buildup. The Allied conference at Yalta is generally seen as the beginning of the Cold War bipolarization. There, the US and USSR agreed on the post-war division of Germany and carved out spheres of influence in the newly liberated European territories (Leffler, 1992).

At the end of the war, the US accounted for more than half of the world's total economic output. It was the only major industrial power left untouched by the war, and its armies controlled most of the globe. It was the most powerful country in the most powerful position the world had ever seen. The US also had a nuclear monopoly. The US had invented nuclear weapons and used them in Japan at the end of the war. All quickly understood that the amazing and horrific power of atomic weapons changed warfare and gave the US an unparalleled strategic capability that it alone in the world could unleash.

As US and Soviet troops met in the middle of Germany, each occupied half of Europe. In the West, the US rebuilt capitalist markets and democratic governments. In the East, the Soviets constructed a series of communist economies and communist governments. The USSR had been invaded twice in twenty years by Germany and wanted to build a zone of security. These conflicting goals quickly led toward confrontation. For example, in Poland, the US and UK wanted to install an exiled democratic government from London to ensure democracy in Poland and a Westward tilt in Polish policies. The Soviets wanted a government in Poland friendly to the USSR, since Poland was the path to invasion of Russia. This meant a communist regime. There was little room to compromise, and with Soviet troops on the ground in Poland, the Soviets prevailed. The US and the USSR, the two power centers left after the war, had radically different views on how the world should be ordered. Moreover, the actions taken by one to ensure security were seen as threatening by the other. They rapidly slid from allies to enemies.

The years 1946-1948 were difficult and tumultuous in world politics. The Grand Alliance that had won the war was coming under severe strain as the diplomats tried to implement the post war plans. Aware that early efforts under the Bretton Woods system to rebuild European economies were not enough, the US proposed the Marshall Plan to help rebuild Europe. The US placed a significant condition on this aid, however, insisting on multilateral cooperation by the applicant countries. This was a major turning point in that it solidified the Western Bloc economically. The Soviet Union declined to participate in the program and instructed its newly created satellites to opt out as well. Thus, Europe was split in two (Leffler, 1992).

The US–Soviet conflict was defined by two different approaches to world order. The Soviet Union sought to develop a set of communist satellites controlled by one-party totalitarian regimes. Each satellite was to be loyal, controlled and shaped by Moscow. The United States, on the other hand, sought to create an international order of liberal democracies, joined by an open international economic order (Ruggie, 1984, 1997). These two visions of world order came into direct conflict, as states had to choose either one or the other. It was not possible to split the difference, so to speak, as communism and capitalism demanded a radically different ordering of society.

BIPOLARITY

Immediately after the war, the United States had a globally deployed army and navy, a nuclear monopoly, and a roaring economy and industrial base left untouched by combat. Yet, immediately after the war, there was a massive demobilization and a transition back to a peacetime economy that caused a recession. The Soviet military was deployed in large numbers in Europe, outnumbering US forces there. The Soviets, however, had been devastated by the war, incurring tremendous population losses, as well as losing most of their industrial base west of the Urals. Each side rapidly transformed its military posture to address the threat posed by the other. In 1949 the USSR detonated its own atomic bomb, making the conflict nuclear. Knowing that it was at a numerical disadvantage in Europe, the US relied on its superior nuclear position and threatened massive retaliation to any Soviet move against the West. This meant that any direct conflict between the two superpowers would rapidly go nuclear, and that would be devastating. Each war scare thus carried with it the possibility of complete nuclear annihilation.

Nuclear weapons cemented the bipolarization of world politics. With each side's massive military augmented by the awesome destructive power of nuclear weapons, the two poles became the anchors for the development of a bipolar international system. Much of the rest of the world organized into two camps, allied with either East or West. The blocs solidified as each superpower demonstrated both control over its allies and a willingness to intervene globally to protect its reach. This first happened in Korea, where the USSR authorized the North's invasion of the South. The US led an international force to repel the invasion, but when China joined the battle on the side of the North, the Korean War became the first of many cold war dominated international conflicts. 1956 cemented the dominance of each superpower over its bloc. The US forced Britain, France, and Israel to withdraw from Egypt and the Suez, upset with the invasion. The USSR intervened to crush an uprising in Hungary.

The bipolar system was unique in international relations up to that point. The world had seen hegemony from nineteenth-century Britain and sixteenth-century Spain. The world had seen a multipolar balance of power in Europe. Yet these systems were not truly global—they mostly occupied the great powers of Europe and their colonies, leaving vast tracts of the world untouched. But never had the world seen such power with such a global reach as it had in the cold war. The US and USSR carved up the entire world; nothing in international politics escaped the cold war. Three rules made the bipolar system function: containment, deterrence, and proxies. These concepts guided much of defense planning and foreign policy in the Cold War.

Containment was the US grand strategy to fight the cold war. George Kennan, the author of the containment policy, drafted a grand strategy that would last for 45 years. His logic was simple. Soviet communism, he reasoned, needed to expand to survive. If it could be contained by the United States, it would collapse under its own weight. The US decided to restrict the space into which the Soviets could extend communist influence. Moreover, if communism spread, it would infect nearby nations, and entire regions could fall to communism like a row of dominoes. Therefore, it was imperative for the US to build a bulwark of allied states around the Soviet Union to contain its expansion as well as intervene globally wherever communism threatened to take root. As a result, the US felt it necessary to counter Soviet influence everywhere and anywhere in the world. Containment and its corollary, the domino theory, served as the underlying logic for decades of active US intervention in global affairs and the domestic affairs of other countries.

Initially unsure how to handle the nuclear aspects of the cold war, the bipolar system came to rely on deterrence to keep the peace. Each side built hundreds of nuclear weapons—not to use in an offensive capacity, but to use as a threat of retaliation for any attack. The threat of nuclear retaliation was designed to deter the other side from taking any offensive action. This logic fed into a nuclear arms race with the advent of MAD— Mutually Assured Destruction. Each side built so many weapons that it could destroy the other if attacked. Thus, any initial attack would bring about the total destruction of the system, making aggression suicidal. This perverse logic slowly led to the stability of the cold war. The Cuban Missile Crisis showed just how precarious the nuclear balance was. With both sides creeping toward confrontation over the Soviet placement of nuclear weapons in Cuba, the American and Soviet leaders realized that any conflict would certainly become nuclear and certainly devastate, if not destroy, the entire world. Nuclear weapons could threaten and deter. But, the superpowers could not actually fight each other, for any hot war would end the system. As a result, deterrence kept a bipolar peace and led to the polarization of smaller regional conflicts.

Unable to directly confront each other, the superpowers intervened in the developing world, overlaying a global bipolar logic on local struggles. Each side sponsored a set of client states that fought each other in a series of proxy wars. Each side provided aid—economic and military—to states or movements that would ally with them. The cold war fueled civil wars and regional conflicts worldwide. The goal was prestige. The nuclear deterrent of each meant that the global balance of power wasn't really altered by the defection of recruitment of allies. Indeed, the allies brought relatively little military value to the conflict. Rather, the value of allies was positioning—both geographical and rhetorical. Geographically, allies provided bases. But, as the superpowers developed ICBMS, nuclear submarines, and satellites, the geography became less of an issue. In the early 1960's, it was a mortal threat to security that the US had missiles in Turkey and the USSR had missiles in Cuba. By the 1970's, those forward bases were obsolete, as either superpower could launch enough missiles to destroy the entire world several times over. Instead, expanding a bloc was a rhetorical victory, points to be scored in yet another proxy contest between the two superpowers who were too strong to fight each other.

One poignant example of how the bipolar system intervened in regional conflicts is the series of wars between Ethiopia and Somalia. Initially, Ethiopia was pro-US and received US weapons and aid to fight Soviet-supported Somalia. After several coups, Ethiopia became a pro-Soviet state, giving the USSR a minor victory in the struggle for global prestige. As a result, the Somali government was able to turn to the US and win massive aid for its newfound allegiance. Bipolarization forced combatants to pick one patron or the other for aid and assistance. The superpowers cared less about the outcome of the war and people affected by the fighting, and more about the relationship of that conflict to the superpower confrontation— did the US or the USSR-backed state win?

THE COLD WAR AND THE GLOBAL AGENDA

Bipolarity set the global agenda, diverting the world's attention away from many of the issues first proposed in the articulation of the post-World War II international order. The most dramatic bipolarization of local politics were the three split societies' victim of the proxy wars. Germany, Korea, and Vietnam were all artificially split as the direct result of bipolar politics. Germany was the first victim of the Cold War, as four occupying powers could not agree on what to do with the territory under their control. The three Western allies combined their zones of occupation into a new state, one that was immediately brought into the Western alliance. The split city of Berlin became a hot trigger spot of the cold war. Korea was divided by the armistice that ended the war, creating a communist North and capitalist South, a division that has outlived the bipolar world that created it. Vietnam was also divided as the superpowers intervened in a struggle of national liberation to create a communist North and capitalist South.

Many anti-colonial struggles were corrupted by the cold war. The various revolutionary movements, struggling governments, and colonial powers became entangled in the cold war. Any rebel group knew that it could turn to the opposite patron of its government for support, and it often did. Civil wars, such as that in Angola, once fueled by the cold war, still remain unresolved to this day.

The cold war intervened in regional struggles to make them part of the bipolarization, even if that's not what they were originally about. Both the Arab–Israeli and India–Pakistan conflicts became the objects of bipolarization. Each superpower took a side, and each party had an eager weapons supplier and patron. Bipolarization had a dual effect on regional conflicts: arms flowed into each region, allowing for ready resupply and continued warfare using conventional arms. But the superpowers' nuclear umbrella also but a damper on the conflict—the superpowers would intervene to keep it from getting out of control and launching a wider war. An instructive case in point is the 1973 Middle East war. With arms supplied by the Soviet Union, Syria and Egypt were able to rebuild their forces following their 1967 defeat. Similarly, Israel upgraded its forces with a steady supply of US arms. This made the 1973 war possible. As the war grew tense, each side asked its patron for shipments of new arms. This superpower intervention threatened to bring the superpowers into a direct conflict, and they thus intervened to stop the war. The US, in particular, used its arms supplies to move the conflict to a stalemate and end, but only after a nuclear alert in response to Soviet moves. Once again, bipolarization shaped a conflict fundamentally about something else.

Upset with the influence of bipolarization on their affairs of state, a number of developing countries banded together to form a non-aligned movement. Ostensible to counter the leverage of the Eastern and Western blocs, the non-aligned movement nonetheless fell victim to bipolarization. The developing nations needed the economic resources of one superpower or the other. Nonaligned leaders such as India and Egypt still played the bipolar game. India bought arms from and traded with the USSR because its rivals Pakistan and later China were in the US camp. Egypt sought Soviet assistance in arms to fight Israel, and later turned to the US for aid as it sought peace. The group of 77 nonaligned nations, the G-77, played only a minor role in world politics. Its greatest influence was felt in the UN.

Following World War II, the UN was envisioned as the protector of peace and security in the world. The first real chance to exercise this power came in 1948 when North Korea invaded South Korea. The Security Council considered the matter and authorized a US-led UN force to repel the invasion, setting off the Korean War. This could happen only because the Soviet delegate was boycotting the Security Council to protest the fact that US-aligned Taiwan was holding USSR-aligned China's seat at the UN. So, the US could push through resolutions on Korea. When the Soviet delegate returned, he vetoed the resolutions authorizing the UN to continue operations in Korea. The UN Security Council was paralyzed by bipolarization, as each side vetoed the other's proposals. Thus, the UN Security Council became yet another forum for the superpower conflict. It could address only issues on which the two sides agreed, and, under bipolarization, such issues were few and far between.

The global development was also stalled. Bipolarization meant not just two competing security systems, but two competing economic systems as well. The Western system followed the principles of the Bretton Woods system developed after the war. The Soviet system, the ComEcon, offered a communist recipe for global development. The developing countries of the world, many already client states or the site of a proxy war, received development assistance more due to security concerns that economic ones. The primary concern was maintaining bloc cohesion, and economic assistance was yet another way to cement loyalty to the patron superpower.

THE LEGACY OF BIPOLARIZATION

The legacy of the bipolar world system is profound. Though it disappeared over a decade ago, it still influences contemporary global politics in many ways. Indeed, much of the technology that has produced today's globalized world of instant communication and commerce is the product of the cold war. Satellite communication, which today links the globe, making it possible to call anywhere at any time, as well as have global television link-ups, is the product of the bipolar space race. The internet, often considered the driver of a new global culture and communication, is the product of US military scientists attempting to devise a computer network that could survive a nuclear war. E-mail emerged as an added bonus, and has evolved to an essential application.

The cold war even shaped the way we think about the world. Issues from the bipolar world permeated IR scholarship, shaping the central debates on the structure of world politics. Much American IR scholarship was motivated by and used in the Cold War. Thomas Schelling brought game theory and a rational discussion of strategic interaction to international relations theory in an attempt to develop ways to fight a nuclear war (Schelling 1960). The entire concept of Mutually Assured Destruction relies, in many ways, on Schelling's game theory contributions. Schelling's use of the Prisoners Dilemma, Chicken, and other games of strategy have been incredibly influential in shaping contemporary IR theory, and it is the direct result of policymakers looking for additional intellectual capital to fight the cold war. Kenneth Waltz, the father of neorealism, which remains the dominant theory of international politics, was also a product of the bipolar system (Waltz 1979). Waltz's argument in favor of bipolarity and the importance of nuclear weapons in maintaining the balance of power articulated a scientific and theoretical argument to explain the stability of the bipolar system. Its parsimony and power have shaped the field in the years since its publication.

Some scholars even argue that the period of bipolarization should be considered a "long peace" (Gaddis, 1987). They argue that, since 1945, there have been over 50 years of peace among the great powers, an unprecedented absence of major systemic war in the history of world politics. This argument asserts that the bipolar system was uniquely stable in that it provided two rational superpowers to manage international politics. Nuclear deterrence induced rationality—the enormous stakes of any superpower conflict forced leaders to rationally evaluate all policy options. The two sides never came to blows, and, from this perspective, deterrence worked. The superpowers were able to resolve the most threatening issues to world peace in a way that assured an absence of systemic warfare, sparing the world the horrors of previous world wars. As mentioned above, all significant global conflicts were influenced by the cold war in some way. This kept them from spiraling out of control. The bipolar system provided stability unmatched by any other arrangement of world politics (Waltz 1979).

But the price of that stability was high. The cost of maintaining the bipolar system bankrupted and ultimately destroyed the USSR, leaving it significantly poorer today than it was at the height of the cold war. Maintaining nuclear deterrence kept the world on hair-trigger alert, and the US and Russia maintain a largely cold-war-style nuclear deterrent that could still wreak global destruction. But the price of the bipolar system was largely paid by the developing world. Millions died in the proxy wars of the bipolar system. Human development suffered as the superpowers competed for security advantages. Today, the developing world is left with a tremendous hangover from bipolarization that continues to be a drag on progress an development. There are literally thousands of weapons circulating worldwide, firepower originally supplied by the superpowers to their clients. The USSR produced so many Kalashnikov rifles that today they are cheaper and more plentiful than a loaf of bread in many poorer parts of the world. These weapons continue to fuel civil wars and regional conflicts. Angola's civil war was polarized and exacerbated by cold war intervention and has yet to be completely resolved. The Korean peninsula remains the last frozen cold war conflict, separated between a communist North and capitalist South. Tensions there remain high to this day. Cuba still endures a stifling embargo by the US, another legacy of Cuba's onetime leading role in the bipolar confrontation. Even the terrorist network of Afghanistan—one of today's most pressing security problems—traces its roots to the cold war. The Soviet invasion prompted the subsequent US support of resistance fighters as proxies. Some of those fighters are today's Taliban and Al Qaeda, using US-supplied weapons in their campaign of global terrorism. It is part of the legacy of bipolarization that we are still trying to overcome.

BIBLIOGRAPHY

Gaddis, John Lewis. 1987. *The Long Peace*. New York: Oxford University Press.

Leffler, Melvyn. 1992. *A Preponderance of Power*. Stanford: Stanford University Press.

Ruggie, John. 1983. "International regimes, transactions, and change: embedded liberalism in the postwar economic order." In *International Regimes*, ed. Stephen Krasner. Ithaca: Cornell University Press.

Ruggie, John. 1997. "The Past as a Prologue? Interests, Identity, and American Foreign Policy," *International Security* 21:4. pp. 89-125

Schelling, Thomas. 1960. *The Strategy of Conflict*. Cambridge, MA: Harvard University Press.

Schweller, Randall. 1998. *Deadly imbalances*. New York: Columbia University Press.

Waltz, Kenneth. 1979. *Theory of International Politics*. Reading, MA: Addison Wesley.

VII
THE COLD WAR
AND AFTER

At the height of the cold war, few could conceive of its end. The bipolar world order appeared highly stable, nuclear deterrence seemed to work, and the superpowers looked so powerful that few could conceive of any course of events that might significantly change the global order (Hutchings, 1997). The only conceivable source of change was an apocalyptical war that would eliminate one or both of the cold warriors, leaving horrific destruction in its path. And yet such a war never came to pass. The cold war ended with a whimper, not a bang, and quickly, quite unexpectedly. In 1988, no major international relations scholar, no major global policy maker, was able to make a credible argument that the cold war was about to end. And yet it did, much to the surprise of observers and practitioners on both sides.

Looking back, the evolution of cold war history points to its eventual decline, but at the time, few truly appreciated the significance of what was going on. This in and of itself is significant, because it shows that none of the major schools of thought at the time could predict the most significant change in world politics in the second half of the twentieth century. Why did the cold war end? This is a very important question, one with theoretical, historical, and political consequences. A deeper understanding of the debate surrounding the end of the cold war shows the difficulty of conceptualizing change in world politics.

The debate over the end of the cold war can roughly be divided into two camps, those who look primarily to material causes and those who look to ideational causes. The first camp is the materialists. The materialists look to the balance of power, the distribution of resources, production, technology, and other material factors (Wohlforth, 1996; Brooks and Wohlforth, 2000-2001). Theoretically, they tend to be realists. They generally tend to argue that the United States outlasted, out spent, and out produced the Soviet Union, driving it into the ground. On the other side, the ideationalists look to a change in the ideas and norms that constitute international politics. They generally tend to argue that new ideas infiltrated the Eastern Bloc and undermined it from within (Koslowski and Kratochwil, 1995; Checkel, 1997; Fierke, 1998). The rise of human rights, glasnost, perestroika, and other ideational concepts changed the way the USSR thought about its security and made new actions possible. This new possibility ended the cold war. Both approaches contain significant diversity, but the general distinction between the two highlights the ongoing debate over the end of the cold war. A more in-depth review of each story reveals the significant differences of each explanation.

THE MATERIAL STORY

In the 1950's, Krushchev famously banged his shoe on the podium of the UN General Assembly and said "We will bury you!" He was referring to the high rates of post-war economic growth enjoyed by the communist bloc compared with the low rates of growth in the capitalist countries. The centralized Soviet economy rapidly rebuilt heavy industry and military production after the second World War. Over the long run, however, this proved not to be the case. The Soviet economy slowed, and by the 80's, Soviet economic growth was minimal. Market-driven economies proved to be much more efficient and flexible in adjusting production priorities in response to changes in demand. Western Europe eventually became a vibrant market and a global economic powerhouse. The US economy, thriving in the 1960's, went through a rough period of inflation and recession in the late 70's and early 80's. But, by the mid-80's, the US had recovered economically, though retaining its large debt.

This economic performance is vital to the cold war because of the arms race. The cold war was dominated by a military struggle between the superpowers, with each building a bigger, faster, and deadlier military force. Although the two sides never fought in combat, they did compete. The earliest competition was to build a nuclear arsenal and the H-bomb. Then came the space race and the competition to develop a fleet of intercontinental ballistic missiles. These efforts required substantial investments of science, technology, military production, and state spending. The arms control agreements of détente in the 70's did little to slow the arms race—instead they added fuel to the fire. The SALT treaties placed limits on each side's nuclear arsenal, but limits that each side had to build up to. To comply with the treaty's limits, each side needed to build more weapons.

The early 80's marked an aggressive posture by the US in the Cold War. US President Reagan came to office with a get-tough approach to the cold war and increased US involvement, both covertly and overtly, in confronting the Soviets on a wide range of issues. In the early 80's, the Reagan spent billions of dollars on a massive defense build-up and ran up trillions of dollars in debt. The US poured billions of dollars into the military, buying new high-technology weapons. The 80's brought about a new technological race for the cold war, space-based missile defense (FitzGerald, 2000). This missile shield threatened to render nuclear deterrence obsolete, but at the cost of trillions of dollars.

In many respects, the beginning of the end of the cold war came in 1985 when Mikhail Gorbachev assumed power in the USSR. The USSR was in dire straits in the mid 1980's. Its economy was crippled, and had been for some time, and it could not afford the costs of the cold war. Gorbachev sought ways to reduce the Soviets' need to compete with the US. Arms control talks shifted from SALT to START, from a limit on nuclear weapons to the actual reduction of nuclear weapons. When Reagan and Gorbachev finally met to negotiate arms control agreements, they, in 1987, signed the INF treaty, which eliminated an entire class of nuclear weapons. Reagan kept pushing for further cuts, and Gorbachev was willing to opt out of the expensive competition. At one point, Gorbachev offered to get rid of all nuclear arms in exchange for Reagan giving up Star Wars, a move that might save the Soviet Union, but Reagan would not do it. The USSR had lost the ability to keep up with the US militarily, and its attempts to do so only sapped the Soviet economy and pushed it farther behind.

To reform the communist system, Gorbachev instituted his policies of glasnost, which meant "openness." He was trying to open up Soviet society and change how the USSR operated to save the system itself. This led him to agree to dramatic changes in the US-USSR relationship (Gorbachev, 2002). It is sufficient to say that when Gorbachev gave his so-called "Sinatra speech" (let them do it their way), renouncing the Brezhnev doctrine of intervening to protect communist governments in Eastern Europe, the cold war ended. The USSR could no longer protect its sphere of influence in Eastern Europe. Poland's government changed to an elected Solidarity government and turned from the East to the West. Hungary opened up its borders, and finally, in 1989, the Berlin wall fell. Soon, all the former communist governments of Eastern Europe were gone. Hardliners in the USSR attempted a failed coup, trying to depose Gorbachev, and on Dec 25, 1991, the USSR fell apart (Beschloss and Talbott, 1993). The cold war was over.

This story emphasizes the growth in material production of the United States (Brooks and Wohlforth, 2000-2001) and the decline of the material power of the Soviet Union. As the US economy grew, it could spend a smaller percentage of GNP on defense. The openness of the economy allowed for both private and public investment in new technologies that then produced a more powerful military force. The US could thus fight the cold war, run up a multi-trillion dollar debt, but still retain a thriving and growing domestic economy. The USSR, on the other hand, could not. Centralized planning stifled development and required a greater and greater share of the economy be devoted to defense needs. The early expansion of the communist sphere of influence provided resources for the growth of the Soviet economy, but containment and the Sino-Soviet split eliminated this source of growth. The Soviets could not afford to develop the technology and infrastructure for the next generation of space-based and stealthy cold war weapons. The economy collapsed under the burden of the cold war and ended the superpower standoff by eliminating a superpower.

THE IDEATIONAL STORY

The ideational story traces the end of the cold war to other causal factors. Instead of the tracing the bipolar nature of the material balance of power, the ideational story examines the breakdown in the rules that governed the cold war, both internationally and domestically. These rules started to break down by the late 70's, and into the 1980's.

The first change came with the greater attention to human rights—the internal practices of states in relation to their own people—on the international agenda. This began with the signing of the Helsinki Final Acts in 1975. These treaties were the final settlement of WWII, and served to fix borders in Europe. The significance of the acts is that they included human rights as one "basket" of the international agreement. They overtly linked state sovereignty and the alteration of borders with the observation of human-rights norms. Having made this commitment, the communist bloc came under criticism by both other states and their own people about how they treated their own citizens. The acts led to the proliferation of human rights groups on both sides of the Iron Curtain and human rights became a legitimate cold war point of dispute—not just internationally, but internally. Dissidents within Eastern bloc countries could point to their treatment and demand that their governments respect the treaties they had signed. It made it all the more difficult for the USSR to stifle internal dissent because doing so delegitimized its standing as a signatory to the Helsinki accords.

The failure of the Soviet economy and the numerous succession crises in the early 80's opened the opportunity for new ideas about how to run the Soviet Union to come to the fore (Checkle 1997). In 1985, Mikhail Gorbachev came to power in the USSR with the goal of reforming the struggling Soviet political and economic system. He adopted policies of political openness and economic restricting—glasnost and perestroika. These policies marked a significant departure from the past policies of autocratic central control by Moscow of both the USSR and its Eastern European satellites. They opened political space for dissident groups within the Soviet bloc to criticize the government.

The rules of the international game changed as well. The Reagan and Gorbachev arms talks created a new realm of possibility for superpower relations in Europe (Fierke, 1998). Once competitive in a zero-sum game, Europe became a more cooperative forum where the two leaders and two sides could negotiate for the betterment of the common good. Removing intermediate range missiles from Europe became a possible fair trade, whereas before it would have been a victory for one over the other.

These changes led to a rethinking of the Cold War. Eastern European satellites and Soviet republics, long under the strict control of Moscow, were given more control over their political and economic lives. This degraded the cohesiveness of the Soviet Bloc, and in 1989, a series of Eastern European countries opened their political process. In Poland, the Solidarity movement successfully challenged the communist government, and Moscow agreed to let the challenge stand, whereas a decade earlier they had threatened military intervention to resist

Solidarity. The Hungarian government opened its borders to the West, allowing thousands to emigrate. East Germany, overwhelmed by the pressure of people seeking to move West, relaxed its border guard, allowing people to cross the Berlin Wall unchecked. As a result, citizens took to the street and knocked down the wall, ending the separation between East and West Germany. Communists lost democratic elections in Poland, East Germany, and Czechoslovakia and peacefully handed over power (Koslowski and Kratochwil, 1995). The Cold War was over.

In 1991, the constituent Republics of the Soviet demanded greater autonomy, and sought to renegotiate the original treaty of union. After a failed coup, the republics challenged the legitimacy of the Soviet government and broke away. On December 25, 1991, the Soviet Union collapsed when Russian military commanders decided to consider orders from Russian President Boris Yeltsin more legitimate than those of the deposed Soviet leaders. The world woke up the next day and the USSR was gone. The buildings, tanks, missiles and uniforms remained the same, but the ideas that had held the Soviet empire together for 74 years had ceased to have any political legitimacy to command respect and allegiance.

SIGNIFICANCE

Why does the debate between these two stories matter (Hogan, 1992)? It is significant for two reasons: first how to understand change in international relations, and second, how to understand the most pressing issues of the post-cold war world. From a theoretical perspective, the ongoing debate over what ended the cold war highlights the different ways to conceptualize change within the international system. The materialist story is familiar to all as a framework for world politics—change only comes as power shifts. The ideational story is a bit more nuanced, locating change in the way in which people come act on shared ideas about what is legitimate and acceptable. Change comes as shared ideas and people's shared views of those ideas evolve to demand a new type of social action. The two views of change offer alternative paths for studying the evolution of the international system, locating the main causes of significant international events, and understanding the importance of present and future events.

Which story is more convincing? Each has its strengths. Certainly the Soviet Union crumbled from within. By the end, its economy was in shambles, its military sat on top of a house of cards that collapsed with one blow. Yet, the material distribution of power in the world was not all that different in January 1992 than December 1991. The most significant events at the end of the cold war had little to do with material capabilities at all. The opening of borders, free elections, decisions to defect from the Soviet side to the Russians—all were decisions taken in the name of ideas and ideologies, not material factors. Both stories are important in telling some of the tale. The complete history requires a melding of both approaches. But, the contemporary study of world politics demands that scholars and practitioners alike privilege one version over the other.

From a practical perspective, this debate is important because it indicates what the most pressing issues are in the post-cold-war world. The materialist camp would assess today's world order as hegemony based on superior US material capabilities. The biggest concern in that order is the rise of other material power centers—WMD proliferation. The ideationalist camp would assess the contemporary order as one based on a set of rules for governance, and that the underpinnings of US hegemony are cultural. The legitimacy of this governance is thus the most pressing issue in world politics. The eventual compromise in this debate colors the visions of the post-cold-war world.

THE PROMISE AND FAILURES OF THE END OF THE COLD WAR

By 1992, the USSR and was gone, replaced by multiple successor states. The Soviet vision of world order had crumbled, leaving the US-led system of global governance (Bush and Scowcroft, 1998), which is largely based on the Post-WWII architecture (Clark, 2001). At the center of this system is the UN. The immediate aftermath of the cold war produced a resurgence of the UN in world affairs. For years, the US and USSR had deadlocked the security council with dueling vetoes. But, with this standard disagreement gone, the UN has found a freedom to act on a host of new issues, and the UNSC emerged from deadlock to function as it was originally intended to do. The immediate post-cold-war world was a reassertion of the UN as a major leader in maintaining world order. There was a massive increase in UN peacekeeping and UN-led activities to resolve conflicts worldwide. In the 1991 Persian Gulf War, the UN acted to condemn aggression by Iraq when it invaded Kuwait. The UN authorized sanctions and the use of force and has monitored the illegal weapons programs since. This was the UN returning to its pre- and early Korean War days as the sole authorizer of the legitimate use of force on the international stage. The UN also launched multiple missions to help rebuild failed states—the UN helped Mozambique resolve its civil war, establish a peaceful transition to democratic governance, and move on.

But, today, other factors have cropped up that pose new and interesting issues. The end of the cold war unleashed tremendous global growth for the international economy. This tidal wave of globalization swept across the world to fill in the vacuum left by global security concerns. Nations focused on expanding trade, the international financial markets, and global lines of production. A new emphasis on regional economic accords arose in the likes of NAFTA, APEC, and the EU. The global economy became a dominant force in world politics.

The end of the cold war also opened up a new political space for formerly repressed agendas. Local nationalism, political Islam, ethnic conflicts, and identity politics all arose after the cold war. In the past, parties in these disputes would have become embroiled in cold war proxy conflicts. The cold war had put a lid on many regional and civil wars that smoldered under the boots of the superpowers. With the cold war gone and the threat of superpower intervention removed, these local conflicts could proceed. This led to the eruption of numerous intra-state disputes and civil wars. One of the most notable was the disintegration of the former Yugoslavia. Communism had kept a multi-ethnic Yugoslavia together, and when communism disappeared, the country lost its unifying logic. Leaders turned to ethnic and religious identity to replace communism as a source of political legitimacy, turning one group against another. The country fell apart and into a deadly series of wars. Less dramatically, the Czechs and Slovaks decided to split, dividing their country in half. Such an event would have been impossible during the cold war, but was easily part of the post-cold-war world.

The end of the superpower rivalry also opened the way for new actors to emerge on the world stage. China and India, the two largest countries in the world, found a new voice as regional and global powers. A reunified Germany assumed a much greater voice in both Europe and the world (Zellikow and Rice, 1995). The European Union emerged as a single market and economic actor. The openness of the post-cold-war world also allowed non-traditional players in world politics to emerge. NGOs and other non-state actors have been able to use the tools of globalization to advance their agenda in previously unfathomable ways.

These events have challenged the global political order in many ways, but, the post-World War II order remains the only way to deal with most contemporary issues of world politics. The global economy still rests on the norms and institutions of the Bretton Woods regime: the IMF, World Bank, and WTO. The UN still serves as the forum for resolving international disputes, legitimizing international uses of force or sanctions, and addressing major international crises. It is far from a perfect order, but, to date, no alternative has replaced it.

The closest alternative order is that of American hegemony. While the USSR crumbled after 1991, the United States grew tremendously in the decade following the cold war. The US economy grew at an amazing rate, producing incredible gains in wealth, technology, and trade. US military capabilities and technology were able to capitalize on this, forming an unparalleled fighting force that far outclasses even its closest allies, let alone its nearest competitors. In many respects, the US is the "indispensable nation," as former Secretary of State Madeline Albright once said, because most international issues cannot be adequately addressed without considering the US position and participation. Economically, no one has wealth that the US does. Militarily, no one has the global reach, transport, communications, intelligence, and precision munitions that the US does. Socially, no one has the powerful cultural draw in both values and consumption that the US does.

But, what is the most important aspect of contemporary American hyperpower? How might this power reshape the world order? The direction of that change depend on how one assesses the most underlying factors of US hegemony and global change. Is it the material power of the American military? Is it the ideational attraction of US institutions and culture? Is it the power of the US economy? Is it a combination of all three? Understanding how this order operates and how it might change, though, depends on having a well developed understanding of change—what causes change in the international system.

The debate between the materialists and ideationalists is one that will not be settled anytime soon. Indeed, both positions have merit and are essential to understanding the end of the cold war and rise of the contemporary international order. But, it is important to note that each prescribes a different vision of international change, and that vision can lead one to radically different policies, actions, and assessments in world politics. The end of the cold war was certainly one of the most important changes in international politics in the past 20 years, but the source, importance, and meaning of that change depends entirely on the theoretical outlook one adopts.

BIBLIOGRAPHY

Beschloss, Michael and Strobe Talbott. 1993. *At the Highest Levels.* Boston: Little, Brown.

Brooks, Stephen and William Wohlforth. 2000-2001. "Power, Globalization, and the End of the Cold War: Reevaluating a Landmark Case for Ideas," *International Security* 25:3, Winter. pp. 5-53.

Bush, George and Brent Scowcroft. 1998. *A World Transformed.* New York: Knopf.

Checkel, Jeffrey. 1997. *Ideas and International Political Change.* New Haven: Yale University Press.

Clark, Ian. 2001. *The Post-Cold War Order: The Spoils of Peace.* Oxford: Oxford University Press.

Fierke, Karin. 1998. *Changing Games, Changing Strategies.* Manchester: Manchester University Press.

FitzGerald, Frances. 2000. *Way Out There in the Blue: Reagan, Star Wars and the End of the Cold War.* New York: Simon & Schuster.

Gorbachev, Mikhail and Zdenek Mlynár. 2002. *Conversations with Gorbachev: On Perestroika, the Prague Spring, and the Crossroads of Socialism.* Translated by George Shriver. New York: Columbia University Press.

Hogan, Michael. 1992. *The End of the Cold War: Its Meaning and Implications.* New York: Cambridge University Press.

Hutchings, Robert. 1997. *American Diplomacy and the End of the Cold War.* Baltimore: Johns Hopkins University Press.

Koslowski, Ray and Friedrich Kratochwil. 1995. "Understanding Change in International Politics: The Soviet Empire's Demise and the International System," in *International Relations Theory and the End of The Cold War*, ed Richard Ned Lebow and Thomas Risse-Kappen. New York: Columbia University Press.

Wohlforth, William. 1996. *Witnesses to the End of the Cold War*. Baltimore: Johns Hopkins University Press.

Zelikow, Philip and Condoleezza Rice. 1995. *Germany Unified and Europe Transformed*. Cambridge: Harvard University Press.

VIII
STABILITY IN
INTERNATIONAL
RELATIONS

How stable are international relations? On the one hand, it seems that we live in tumultuous times, where change is the only certainty, where today's rules are tomorrow's fallacies. The world today is different in ways inconceivable merely 10 or 20 years ago. On the other hand, the more things change, the more they stay the same. Despite all the cosmetic change that dominates the headlines, the underlying structure and rules of world politics are largely unchanged. The important things then remain the important things now, and the rules of who gets what, when and how are still true to form. Which is the case? How is one to understand, judge, and measure stability in international relations?

Before exploring the different ways to view stability in world politics, it is perhaps useful to first explore the concept of stability itself—what does it mean for international relations to remain stable? The question of stability in international politics usually refers to the question of world order—the basic structure of rules that govern the day-to-day international relations among actors. These basic rules are in fact more stable than not, and have remained largely the same over the past 50 years, albeit with significant changes. Yet, many of these supposed significant changes were actually changes within the given world order, not changes to the order itself. To understand stability in international politics, it is important to understand the major theories of world order.

The most basic approach to world order holds that someone sets an international order and then makes it so. Not just any state can do this—only a state powerful enough to implement its own rules and then have the power to enforce them can establish and maintain a global order. Indeed, it is the most powerful state in the system, the hegemon, who can establish a stable order for world politics (Gilpin, 1981; Keohane, 1984). Hegemonic stability theory argues that it is the hegemon who establishes a world order and stabilizes international politics under that order.

From the perspective of stability theory, a simple definition of hegemony is based on aggregate power. Usually determined by share of world GNP, the hegemon has the military and economic strength to shape the course of significant world events and has an interest in nearly all relevant international interactions. The hegemony literature is largely based on 2 cases of hegemony: the golden years of British hegemony in the nineteenth century, and the USA from the end of World War II until the present day. Other scholars have identified other hegemons, like eighteenth century Britain, seventeenth century Holland, and sixteenth century Spain (Wallersein, 1974). Each of these states had the dominant military, technology, and economy of its time, with a global reach and interest in each. They dominated the global economic and political order as the leading states of the day and were the ultimate enforcers of the international rules that they upheld.

Hegemonic stability theory, in its simplest form, states that the international system stabilizes when a hegemon exists to impose order and provide collective goods. It has multiple variants in the different subjects it applies to, but its basic appeal is this simplicity and elegance. This approach views world order as a set of collective goods beset with the free-rider problem. Collective goods, such as freedom of the high seas or open trading markets, work to the benefit of all so long as all participate, but the incentive is always for the individual actor to cheat, reaping the benefits of the collective good without paying for it. Thus, the good is over-used and under provided and withers. The traditional solutions to the tragedy of the commons problem in a domestic setting is to either privatize the commons or provide a set of enforceable laws. Privatization divides up the commons / collective good into individualized parcels that can interact within a free market. Enforceable laws endow a governing authority with the legitimate use of force to ensure that users pay and comply with the requisite rules of maintenance. In an international setting, however, neither solution is possible. One cannot privatize the global commons, and there is no world government to enforce rules. Thus, it is left to the hegemon to patrol the global commons, providing the collective goods. It is so big that it can afford to pay a disproportionate share for collective goods, mitigating the cost of free riders, because it reaps a tremendous reward. Moreover, it is so powerful that it can enforce rules and extract payment, mitigating the damage of free riders. The hegemon is able to do this because of its vast power and its interest in maintaining the system that provides that power.

Hegemonic stability theory is often used to explain world economic order—a hegemon comes along and provides the heavy lifting to establish and maintain an international order. It provides basic global security to protect economic relations (Kindleberger, 1970). It promotes open trade by providing open markets and the ability to take goods from here to there (also security) so that goods and services can travel and be traded. In monetary relations, the hegemon establishes the international financial system and provides a reserve currency and some sort of stability to international monetary relations so currencies can be exchanged. Hegemons set up regimes and/or institutions to deal with all sorts of economic issues.

For example, in the nineteenth century, Great Britain was the global hegemon, providing many collective goods necessary for world order. The British navy, at the time the most powerful in the world, patrolled the oceans making the high seas open for trade. Britain lowered its tariffs on imported goods, serving as the ultimate consumer market in the global economy. The pound sterling was the world's most valuable and stable currency. Britain also served as the critical balancer within the European security system, helping to maintain the concert system that avoided continental wars for the better part of that century. In short, as hegemon, Great Britain established and maintained the nineteenth century world order.

It is important to note that that hegemonic stability theory does not say that there will be perfect peace and stability within a given world order, but it does say that other major powers are irrelevant. For instance, under British hegemony in the nineteenth century, there were other great powers, especially on the European continent, and they fought amongst themselves at times supporting and challenging the international order. But, Britain provided key goods, like a reserve currency and freedom of the seas and security which allowed a great many other transactions to take place. For example, the United States, no close ally of Britain in the nineteenth century, nevertheless prospered under the rules of British hegemony. The US traded extensively with Britain, and the US relied on the power of the British navy to both ensure access on the high seas to foreign markets as well as enforce the Monroe doctrine that kept other European powers from entering the Western hemisphere.

Indeed, some argue an international order's stability depends not just on the existence of a powerful hegemon to enforce it, but the type of order that is being enforced (Ruggie, 1983). Each hegemon brings a different recipe for international order, some more stable than others. Great Britain's hegemonic order of the nineteenth century relied on a mercantile economic regime—open within the British colonial system, but closed to those on the outside. It relied on the balance of power to maintain order within Europe and colonialism to keep order across Africa, the Middle East, and Asia. The order imposed by Nazi Germany on its conquered territory relied on a series of bilateral alliances and trade agreements, each designed to weaken the participant and enrich Germany. The American hegemonic order rests on liberalism in both the economic and political realms. Economically, it opens a system of liberal trade and currency arrangements. Politically, it purports to promote human rights and democracy. These principles give the order more legitimacy than other potential organizing rules, and might explain the resilience and resurgence of US hegemony after the end of the cold war.

Many scholars argue that much of world history can be organized around the rise and fall of various hegemonies (Organski, 1980; Modelski, 1987; Goldstein, 1988) tend to argue that there is a cycle of hegemony where one power rises, establishes order, is challenged, falls in a great war, and then a new hegemon arises. From this perspective, the first world war marked the end of British hegemony. Because there was no hegemon in the interwar years to stabilize the global economy, it sank into depression. Britain was no longer strong enough to act as hegemon and the rising power of the US was unwilling to assume its proper role. Only World War II did the US assume the mantle of hegemony and re-establish a new international order.

Hegemonic stability theory does explain long periods of continuity in the basic order of world politics. However, it is not without its flaws. There are three major holes in the theory that one could identify. The first is that true hegemony is harder to achieve than the theory makes it seem. The theory forces one to identify the most powerful state in the system and examine its hegemonic order. Yet it is rare for the most powerful state to dominate international relations in the way the theory predicts. The US dominated international relations in 1945, and does so today. But, many scholars in the United States observed what they considered a wane in US hegemony in the late 70's and early 80's (Kennedy, 1989). The US seemed to be in significant decline as alternative powers such as Japan and the USSR rose to challenge US global dominance. Similarly, Britain dominated certain aspects of international relations in the nineteenth century but was hardly the dominant force in all aspects of global politics. It was repeatedly challenged by other European powers, notably a rising Germany. Indeed, it is rare, if not unique to the contemporary period, that one power can so dominate international politics in the way that the US does. Previous hegemons might have dominated commerce or technology or the balance of power, but even today, there is no way for the hegemon to manage all aspects of the international system. It is just too big and too complex. A hegemony is an imperfect dominance at best. Thus, a hegemon can only stabilize what it can control, and thus the stability of any given hegemony is limited to a few key areas.

The second critique of hegemonic stability theory comes from the realist camp itself. A realist would argue that hegemony is tantamount to unipolarity, and with a history of a multipolar or bipolar system, there really has never been a true hegemon. The classic realist rejoinder is that any time a state gets big enough to become a hegemon, other states would balance against it and bring it down to a more manageable size. Thus, hegemony is not stable, for the rise of a hegemon provokes a counter-alliance that ultimately leads to a power transition and war (Organski, 1980). The continual rise and fall among states as they compete for hegemony is in fact less stable than one might think. Indeed, many realists see a balanced distribution of power as the most stable arrangement in international politics. Some argued that the bipolarity of the cold war was the most stable of all forms of world order—each side could balance the moves of the other, thus preventing any major shifts or changes in world politics (Waltz 1979). The stability of the post-World War II era could be attributed to the establishment of a stable bipolar order, not US hegemony.

Finally, cooperation, order, and stability could develop and persist without a hegemon. Keohane's recipe for international order and cooperation rested on a regime of international institutions to maintain a stable order (1984). One of Keohane's major points was an attack on hegemonic stability theory—though a hegemon could set up an international order, regimes and institutions could function after a hegemon fell and persist absent a hegemonic enforcement. Cooperation could occur on its own merits and produce stable and institutionalize patterns of international politics. This approach gained currency in response to the supposed US hegemonic decline of the late 70's. Immediately following WWII, the US was clearly a hegemon, with armies spanning the globe, and accounting for more than half of total global production. The US established an economic order, the Bretton Woods system, to manage the global economy. This lasted for the 50's and first half of the 60's, but as the story of the international monetary regime tells, US stature declined, and in 1971, the Bretton Woods regime was partially gutted by the US when it went off the gold standard. This was seen by many as a sign of declining US power relative to the rest of the world. The oil shocks, inflation, recessions, and "malaise" of the 70's and early 80's led to a general notion that the US was in some sort of hegemonic decline (Gilpin, 1981; Kennedy, 1989). The Soviets seemed to be catching up, Japan seemed to be overtaking the US economy, and Europe offered the promise of an entity bigger than the US economy. Yet the basic ideas and institutions of international cooperation, such as the IMF and UN, continued to function and maintain order reasonably well. Thus, a stable international order could exist after hegemony (Keohane, 1984).

Indeed, stable institutionalized cooperative patterns can in fact produce stability in international politics without any hegemon. Scholars of international cooperation noticed that in many cases, international collective goods problems in areas like security or trade yield sub-optimal solutions due to the prisoner's dilemma. Actors are always inclined to seek the lowest common dominator to protect themselves from exploitation. Yet, regular cooperation produces better results for all (Axlerod, 1984; Oye, 1986). By eliminating uncertainty caused by incomplete information and extending the shadow of the future through repeated play, actors can cooperate without fear of exploitation. Thus, relatively stable patterns of institutionalized cooperation, based on tit-for-tat models of reciprocity can produce a stable order of international cooperation that benefits all participants (Goldstein and Freeman, 1990).

This final point opens the door to a deeper critique of hegemonic stability theory—it locates stability only in a stable agglomeration of material power around one state. A first cut in this direction might assert that hegemons can accrue "soft" as well as "hard" power (Nye, 1990). Soft power, the appeal of culture and values, can underpin a hegemonic order just as hard economic and military power does. Thus, Nye was able to argue that, from a soft-power perspective, the hegemonic decline arguments of the 70's and 80's were specious. He argued that the stability of the US-led system rested on the broad appeal of US values such as open markets, human rights, and democratic freedoms. These values did not wane; rather, they appeared triumphant in 1989. Though different in detail and function from their founding, major portions of the Bretton Woods system still govern global economy. The UN remains a central force in legitimating international actions. In that respect, the end of cold war was less of a change in world order than many assert. It was instead the continuation and reassertion of the US-led post-World War II international order, an order based on the triumph of ideas, not material power (Mandelbaum, 2003). In this respect, we've had a stable world for nearly 60 years.

A second, deeper cut from this perspective might argue that stability has little to do with either "hard" or "soft" power, but rather the power of the rules and norms that constitute the international system itself (Wendt, 1999). From this perspective, one can say that the basic rules of international relations have remained quite stable for a number of years. Sovereignty has served as the basic governing principle of world politics since 1647. The nation-state continues to be the primary unit of international politics.

Indeed, rules may change. Colonialism is no longer the appropriate mode of state expansion. States come and go. Prussia, the USSR and Yugoslavia are no more; while Bangladesh, Bosnia, and Uzbekistan have all come into existence. Sovereignty changes in meaning and is not what it was. Today sovereignty has been tied to conditional observance of human rights and other international legal regimes. But, these are changes in content, not form. The basic rules remain the same, and with that, the possible outcomes in world politics likewise remain within a stable and limited realm. These basic concepts have made the rules of the international system relatively stable and predictable.

These rules find their stability in their intersubjective nature. Widespread practice and shared understandings based on these rules provide that stability. No one person, no single event can change such a rule. Instead, these rules can only change with a distinct and continual shift in the regular and expected practices of states and the individuals representing states. Material change alone cannot provide this. Notice the end of the cold war. It was at the same time a massive change and an instance of continuity. States disappeared and were created, a conflict ended, and yet, the basic structure of world politics remained the same. The Soviet Union disappeared and the global rules of the cold war lost their meaning. But, on December 26, 1991, the day after the Soviet Union dissolved, its successor states picked up where it left off. Russia assumed the Soviet's sovereign debt and seat on the UN security council. The new states that emerged from Soviet Central Asia declared their sovereignty. All sought entry into the US-led global economy. As much as the world changed that day, it stayed the same. People may have done different things, but they were still operating by the same rules of international politics.

In this respect, stability lies in the way in which we continue to cling to the ideas that make the world work. Though material power may shift within the system, the meaning given to that power and its role in the system have not changed. States rise and fall, armies triumph and fall, but states still constitute the system and armies still serve the state. It is therefore possible to make the claim that the world order is rather stable and only changes slowly. Sovereignty still prevails. US hegemony has organized and ordered global politics since 1945. True change and volatility will only emerge as these basic concepts are rethought and replaced. It would take the emergence of something like a post-national citizenship (Soysal, 1994) or "virtual" (non-territorial) state (Rosencrance, 1999) to truly upset the stability of the present international system.

It is also possible, though, to find this version of stability lacking. This large-scale "stable" system remains quite hollow. What fills it changes quite rapidly. The rules that give these structures meaning change over time as we ask more and different things of the system. And it is this content that fills the form which has the impact on our lived experience in world politics.

In conclusion, stability in world politics can be considered a question of world order. How one treats stability depends on what level of world order one considers the most important for the organization of world politics. To the extent that one looks to the material distribution of power as the central causal force in international relations, stability comes from a world order imposed by a hegemon to manage the system. If, however, one looks to the meaning that empowers material objects as capabilities and to the rules that constitute the system, stability rests in the shared assumptions about what international relations is and how it operates. The sovereign state system, as the form of world politics, has shown marked stability. The content of that system has evolved and changed significantly since the establishment of the state system in 1647, remaining stable for long periods of time when a state could maintain that order. Stability lies in the lens of analysis that one uses to understand world order and world politics.

BIBLIOGRAPHY

Axelrod, Robert. 1984. *The Evolution of Cooperation*. New York: Basic Books.

Gilpin, Robert. 1981. *War and Change in World Politics*. Cambridge: Cambridge University Press,.

Goldstein, Joshua. 1988. *Long Cycles*. New Haven: Yale University Press.

Goldstein, Joshua and John Freeman. 1990. *Three-Way Street* Chicago: University of Chicago Press.

Kennedy, Paul. 1989. *The Rise and Fall of the Great Powers*. New York: Vintage Books.

Keohane, Robert. 1984. *After Hegemony*. Princeton: Princeton University Press.

Kindleberger, Charles. 1970. *Power and money; the economics of international politics and the politics of international economics*. New York: Basic Books.

Mandelbaum, Michael. 2002. *The Ideas That Conquered the World: Peace, Democracy, and Free Markets in the Twenty-First Century*. New York: Public Affairs.

Modelski, George. 1987. *Long Cycles in World Politics*. Seattle: University of Washington Press.

Nye, Joseph. 1991. *Bound to Lead*. New York, Basic Books.

Organski, A. F. K. and Jacek Kugler. 1980. *The War Ledger*. Chicago: University of Chicago Press.

Oye, Kenneth. 1986. *Cooperation Under Anarchy*. Princeton: Princeton University Press.

Rosecrance, Richard. 1999. *The Rise of the Virtual State*. New York: Basic Books.

Ruggie, John. 1983. "International regimes, transactions, and change: embedded liberalism in the postwar economic order." In *International Regimes*, ed. Stephen Krasner. Ithaca: Cornell University Press.

Soysal, Yasemin. 1994. *Limits of Citizenship*. Chicago: University of Chicago Press.

Wallerstein, Immanuel. 1974. *The Modern World-System*. New York: Academic Press.

Waltz, Kenneth. 1979. *Theory of International Politics*. Reading, MA: Addison Wesley.

Wendt, Alexander. 1999. *Social Theory of International Politics*. Oxford: Cambridge University Press.

IX
WAR

"Why war?" was the original and remains the ultimate question in international relations. It is why many are motivated to study international relations. War, along with sovereignty, is a defining characteristic of world politics, one of the few unique concepts that international relations can claim to separate it from other disciplines. This discussion of war will first look a the definition of the concept itself, then broadly trace the evolution of warfare and its place in shaping international relations, and examine the way in which scholars have begun to answer the question of why war, and finally review the attempts to bring order to the chaos of war.

WHAT IS WAR?

Violence is nearly omnipresent in international relations. Indeed, scanning the headlines on any given day will reveal multiple instances of violence on each and every continent. Governments use force frequently as a tool of diplomacy and to maintain order. But little of this is considered an actual war. Only rarely do societies consider themselves in a state of war, and such states are the exception rather than the rule. What separates war from disputes, from violence, from fighting, and from murder?

War is often thought of as the organized application of violence by one state against another. As a product and part of the international system, war must be carried out at the international level, which means that states or state-like entities must be both the sponsors and targets of war. State-like entities would include groups that act like a state and are seeking either their own status as a state or to capture the government of an existing state. The cost and complexity of modern warfare require the political organization and bureaucratic coordination of a state or quasi-state-like structure.

War must be large in scope. Sporadic or limited violence and death, while tragic in its own right, rarely qualifies as a war. Some scholars (Singer, 1979) have argued that a conflict can only be called a war when each side suffers at least 1000 battle deaths per year. While this is a completely arbitrary number, it reflects the notion that war involves conflict, death, and destruction on the largest scale possible. Smaller conflicts frequently occur, but these limited conflicts are not wars.

War must be organized. While in the abstract, the killing and destruction associated with war may seem pointless and random, states launch wars for particular purposes. As Clausewitz's (1976) famous dictum goes, war is the pursuit of politics by other means. War serves some political purpose, and war fighting is organized to reach that political goal. The violence of war, while seemingly arbitrary in its specific manifestations, is nonetheless organized and directed toward the achievement of a political goal. Such a goal might be survival, preemption, irredentism, or liberation, but regardless of the validity of the project, all wars have political motivation.

THE EVOLUTION OF WAR

War is older than recorded history—as long as has been recounted, societies have fought each other to settle disputes. And, throughout its long history, war has always been brutal. The lethality and devastation wrought by warfare are at once its most consistent and yet changing factors. For as human technology evolved, it has changed the face of warfare, and a desire to gain the upper hand in armed conflict has spurred countless technological and scientific achievements. The development and application of new technology have shaped the evolution of warfare.

Early warfare was highly personal and limited in that a warrior could attack only that which he (and the vast majority of warriors throughout history have been male (Goldstein, 2001) could reach with his own limbs. Wars were, by necessity, limited and local—armies could attack only that which they could march to and over. The development of metals for swords and shields increased the effectiveness of the individual soldier. The development of bronze was one of the first technological changes to the conduct of warfare. The development of the chariot and later the stirrup significantly changed warfare in two ways. First, it added speed and height on the battlefield—a mounted soldier had a significant advantage over one on foot. Second, it increased the range of an army. Mounted troops could travel farther than troops on foot. The horse became an integral part of warfare until the availability of the automobile in the beginning of the twentieth century offered a suitable alternative. The chariot was perhaps the most revolutionary and effective weapon of ancient times. It was the development of innovations such as the long bow and catapult that introduced the notion of stand-off weaponry to warfare. Simply put, these innovations created the opportunity to launch an attack from a distance. Yet even with early stand-off weapons, warfare remained largely a close-encounter affair, where armies fought each other through direct personal combat.

Perhaps the most consequential change in the face of warfare was the development of gunpowder. Gunpowder and explosives rendered all prior military technology obsolete. Armor, once valuable protection against swords, spears, and arrows, was no match for a bullet. Castles and city walls, once nearly impervious protection from catapults and soldiers, fell easily to a cannon blast. Ships could blast each other out of the water. Not only could cannons launch projectiles over greater distances and with greater force, but those projectiles could be explosive themselves. Gunpowder added an element of distance to warfare. With infantry soldiers armed with guns, combat became a shooting match over a distance, moving away from the person-to-person combatant battles of ancient times. Over time, war fighting became organized around explosive technology, and today it dominates the battlefield. Technology developed to create bigger explosions to launch either greater sizes or numbers (or both) of projectiles with increasing accuracy. The pistol, machine gun, and rocket increased the lethality an army could inflict on an opponent.

Throughout much of this history, warfare remained the job of privileged elite, a warring class. The knights of the middle ages fought each other in the name of a king, but the king's subjects themselves did not fight. Many governments relied on mercenaries. These hired soldiers participated in many great battles because governments did not have enough members of the warrior class to conduct effective warfare. It was only with the rise of the modern industrial nation-state that the concept of total war came into existence. The French and American revolutions, in bringing democracy to a people as a system of government, also brought the notion of the mass army, one populated by conscripts drawn from the whole of society (Posen). The French were the first to make wide use of the mass army, and it fueled several early military victories.

The rise of the industrial nation-state substantially changed the nature of warfare. Nationalism could become motivating fuel for a mass citizen army. But, as Tilly notes, just as states make war, war also made states (1975). War required the expansion of the nation state's capabilities and reach. States needed to tax to raise the revenue to pay for war. States needed to keep better records of their populations to manage, recruit, and train them as soldiers. States needed an industrial policy to ensure the development of technologies to resources. And, for many states, service in the armed forces became a key socializing force in forging a national identity among what were previously highly regionalized countries (Weber, 1976). The modern industrial nation-state as we know it is, in many ways, the product of a series of wars and war mobilizations.

The merger of the industrial economy with the stronger governments of modernizing nation-states produced the possibility of total war. Industrial production allowed states to gear whole societies to wartime footing. The two World Wars were the ultimate expression of total war, where an entire state went to war with the total population and institutions of another state.

Since 1945, the advent of nuclear weapons has revolutionized warfare once again. Nuclear weapons have made a total war too costly to fight. Reinforced by the massive nuclear arsenals of the Cold War superpowers, total nuclear war would result in the complete destruction of both sides. The sheer destructive power of nuclear weapons—the ability to wipe entire cities, entire populations, from the face of existence with one bomb or missile—has one again forced a rethinking of warfare. These weapons could threaten, but, ultimately, could not be used in any substantial number for any effective military purpose.

And again, today, there is the emerging notion of a yet another new type of war, the war on terrorism. Here, warfare has broken down the barrier between civilian and combatant, state and society. It is a war where one party is not a state, and operates in the shadows between and within states. It is at once a new type of war taking advantage of the latest in modern technology and society and an old type of war employing a religious / civilizational confrontation that harkens back hundreds of years to a pre-state period (Benjamin and Simon, 2002; Huntington, 1996).

"Why war?" is one of the most fundamental questions of political science, one that has spawned many theories yet few satisfying answers. The following section reviews some of the most significant explanations for why states resort to war to settle a dispute.

One of the earliest answers invoked the fundamental structure of the international system. States go to war because there is nothing to stop it (Waltz, 1959). Sovereignty creates a set of equals with no central authority. Lack of a central authority gives rise to anarchy. Under conditions of anarchy, a state's sovereignty is only as good as its ability to defend its borders. Because no state rules another, no one state has the ability to prevent war. Quite simply, states go to war because they can.

This type of permissive answer, however, is of little practical value—it offers little to explain when wars might occur and why a particular state might launch a war against another.

Subsequent approaches have attempted to be much more specific. One reached back to the writing of Thucydides for an explanation. Thucydides explained the Peloponnesian war by observing that the rise of the power of Sparta struck fear in Athens, bringing the two city-states into a conflict. Power transition has thus been identified as a cause of war (Gilpin, 1981). As one state gains power and another state's power declines, the two states can easily end up in conflict—either the falling state can attempt to preemptively take out its rising competitor, or the rising state may aggressively seek to push the declining state over the edge. The uncertainties and instability created by power transitions have been identified as a fertile ground for war.

Realists who look to the balance of power as the defining characteristic of the international system see war as the result of an imbalance of power. For example, tripolarity—three centers of power in the international system—is particularly unstable as two poles can easily join up to conquer the third (Schweller, 1998). If one state gets too powerful, it can provoke a counterbalancing alliance that will attempt to reduce the large state's influence. With sovereign states in anarchy, war is the ultimate way to settle disputes among states when the balance of power is out of alignment. Thus, any perturbation that interferes with the natural balancing behavior of states can be a cause of war.

Yet, on the eve of World War I, the states of Europe stood aligned in two opposing blocs, each designed to balance the other. This balance did not preserve peace—rather, it was instrumental in the descent into war. Alliances, timetables, and war plans pulled unwitting states into a global war. Many have studied World War I, and some have identified the myths, folly, and misperceptions that led states into war. Nearly all European leaders were under the impression that war would be quick, decisive, and healthy for the continent. The folly of war among leaders led to a senseless stalemate of slaughter on the battlefield (Tuchman). Others argue that certain coalitions capture the state, such as the "Iron and Rye" coalition of farmers and industrialists in Germany. These groups benefit from a war and warlike policies at the expense of the rest of the state, and their coalitions use the state and the state of war to both maintain the coalition and advance its interests (Snyder, 1991).

Democracy might be an answer to such explanations of war—its open political structure and liberal values make it more difficult for any coalition to capture the state in such a way. Indeed, it is well noted that in the history of warfare, democracies do not fight each other (Russett). It is not that democracies are less war-like, they fight non-democracies regularly, but there are no clear cut historical records of democracies fighting other democracies. This democratic peace has several potential sources, ranging from the shared liberal values, to a value on democratic and legalistic procedures of conflict resolution to a shared identity. Yet it has also been observed that democratizing states, those states making the transition from an authoritarian regime to a democratic one, are more war-prone (Mansfield and Snyder, 1995). Thus, while stable democracies share a zone of peace, the transition to democracy can often be violent.

In fact, it is possible for leaders to use war as a diversionary tactic to shift the focus of public opinion from an unpopular issue to a popular war (Levy, 1989). A leader can use a war to shift people's attention, thus solidifying an agenda in a newly ignored area. It is well documented that public opinion naturally rallies around a national leader in a time of crisis (Mueller, 1973). This rally-around-the-flag effect boosts, temporarily, the standing of a leader or leadership group, allowing a war to distract people from other national issues.

The choice for war, however, rarely, if ever benefits a state. Instead, the choice for war is usually disastrous for all involved. Why, then, would a state ever choose to go to war? One obvious answer is that leaders misperceive the situation (Jervis, 1976). Leaders may not see all the potential costs or might misjudge the risks involved in launching a war. A new set of explanations is emerging, however, that show how war might become a seemingly rational choice for a leader to make. War can be a rational decision only when leaders think that they can benefit from a war (Bueno de Mesquita, 1981). This only happens, though, through imperfect information (Fearon, 1995). In a world of perfect information, all would know who is stronger and thus who is more likely to win a war. Thus, given the existing power reality, a negotiated solution could reach the most likely outcome without the devastation of war. Imperfect information skews this process, making it possible for each side to believe, rationally, that war is both winnable and beneficial.

RULES OF WAR

Can war have rules? War has long been defined by cultural practices determining how one should confront an enemy. It is only in modern times that the Western notion of decisive and total victory over an opponent came to dominate the conduct of war (Keegan, 1976). Even in this chaos of war, states have tried to impose and recognize rules of warfare. Repulsed by the violence and suffering he observed on European battlefields, Henry Dunant proposed a set of international humanitarian standards to care for wounded and non-combatants. Dunant's proposal became the Red Cross, and his notions of conduct in warfare were formalized by governments in a series of Geneva Conventions. These conventions govern state conduct in wartime (Finnemore, 1996). The Geneva conventions were the beginning of a significant body of international law governing the conduct of war. It is, for example, illegal to shoot prisoners of war or massacre civilians.

Ultimately, though, these laws of war rely on the willingness of states to abide by them in a reciprocal fashion. In the years after World War I, the world's leaders signed a treaty outlawing war, a treaty that obviously did not last. But, there is a significant history of states following the rules of war. In the First World War, soldiers along the trenches would fall into a pattern of live-and-let-live exchanges of fire with their adversaries (Axelrod, 1984). In the Second World War, opposing armies refrained from deploying chemical weapons. By and large, the Red Cross has been able to inspect prisoner-of-war camps and monitor the conduct of war. Yet, with no international government to enforce such rules, they, like all international laws, rely on reciprocity and continued international cooperation. There is nothing to stop a state from starting a war or breaking the rules of war except for the shadow of the future—the potential of future retribution by other states.

CONCLUSION

War is perhaps the most awful condition that humanity can bring upon itself. War is as old as recorded history and remains part of international relations to this day. War persists because it is still a legitimate tool of statecraft, the ultimate arbiter of disputes in the international system. There are many possible causes of war, though scholars of international politics cannot identify any one definitive cause. War remains the exception, not the rule, of international politics—though there is nothing to stop war from happening, it happens relatively infrequently. But, war remains a central feature of the international system of sovereign states and will remain so for the foreseeable future.

BIBLIOGRAPHY

Axelrod, Robert. 1984. *The Evolution of Cooperation.* New York: Basic Books.

Benjamin, Daniel and Steven Simon. 2002. *The Age of Sacred Terror.* New York: Random House.

Bueno de Mesquita, Bruce. 1981. *The War Trap.* New Haven: Yale University Press.

Fearon, James. 1995. "Rationalist explanations for war," *International Organization* 49:3, Summer. pp. 379-414.

Finnemore, Martha. 1996. *National Interests in International Society.* Ithaca: Cornell University Press.

Goldstein, Joshua. 2001. *War and Gender.* Cambridge: Cambridge University Press.

Huntington, Samuel. 1996. *The Clash of Civilizations and the Remaking of World Order.* New York: Simon and Schuster.

Jervis, Robert. 1976. *Perception and Misperception in International Politics.* Princeton: Princeton University Press.

Keegan, John. 1976. *The Face of Battle.* London: J. Cape.

Levy, Jack S. 1989. "The Diversionary Theory of War: A Critique," in Manus Midlarsky, ed. *Handbook of War Studies.* Ann Arbor, MI: The University of Michigan Press. pp. 259-288.

Mansfield, Edward and Jack Snyder. 1995. "Democratization and the Danger of War," *International Security.* Volume 20, Number 1, Summer. pp. 5-38

Mueller, John. 1973. War, Presidents, and Public Opinion. New York, Wiley.

Posen, Barry R. 1993. "Nationalism, the Mass Army, and Military Power," *International Security*. Volume 18, Number 2, Fall. pp. 80-124

Russett, Bruce. 1993. *Grasping the Democratic Peace*. Princeton: Princeton University Press.

Schweller, Randall. 1998. *Deadly imbalances*. New York: Columbia University Press.

Singer, J. David. 1979. *The Correlates of War*. New York: Free Press.

Snyder, Jack. 1991. *Myths of Empire*. Ithaca, NY: Cornell University Press

Thucydies. 1982. *The Peloponnesian War*. New York, Random House.

Tilly, Charles ed. 1975. *The Formation of National States in Western Europe*. Princeton: Princeton University Press

Tuchman, Barbara. 1962. *The Guns of August*. New York: Macmillan.

Von Clausewitz, Carl. 1976. *On War*. Princeton: Princeton University Press.

Waltz, Kenneth. 1954. *Man, the State, and War*. New York: Columbia University Press.

Weber, Eugen. 1976. *Peasants into Frenchmen*. Stanford, CA: Stanford University Press.

X
CONFLICT RESOLUTION
AND THE SETTLEMENT
OF DISPUTES

Mainstream international relations theories and approaches tend to focus on states, foreign policies, and international conflict. Volumes have been dedicated to explaining the outbreak of major wars or the sources of violent conflicts. Yet even a casual review of history reveals that these conflicts do not continue in perpetuity. At some point, wars end, conflicts are resolved and disputes are settled. While many study the transition from peace to war, it is also worthwhile to study the transition from war to peace.

The field of conflict resolution is a broad amalgamation of insights from psychology, social psychology, anthropology, education, religion, history, economics, law, and political science. In many ways, it is more of an approach to conflict than a distinct field or discipline. Yet, it remains an important and growing approach within international relations. The strengths of the conflict resolution approach are its focus on practical application of knowledge to solve real-world problems and its ability to incorporate non-mainstream ideas from a variety of formal disciplines. Thus, constructivist scholars, non-violent activists, social psychologists, and legal arbiters can all contribute valid and vital knowledge to the study and practice of resolving international disputes.

Conflict resolution is linked to the notion of peace studies—the investigation of peace rather than war. Central to understanding this approach is the working definitions of peace used to motivate study. For much of the field of international relations, peace is no more than the absence of war. In this sense, peace and war are opposite conditions of the international system. The beginning of a cease-fire signals the transition from war to peace. But, when settling disputes, peace becomes a much thicker concept. Parties to a dispute may not feel satisfied or safe just because fighting may have stopped. Moreover, a cease-fire agreement that halts a war rarely addresses the underlying causes of that war. Simply halting violence is no guarantee that violence will not recur in the near future.

In order to distinguish between the mere absence of war and a long-term, stable, peaceful society, conflict resolution distinguishes between a positive and negative peace (Rapoport, 1992). Negative peace is the thin notion of the absence of war and violence. Positive peace, on the other hand, is the thicker notion of relationships based on cooperation and trust. Under a condition of positive peace, states and groups promote a positive social order that protects and respects all its members. Thus, a positive peace is a rational, cooperative and dynamic interaction. A true positive peace will also address not only direct violence, but structural violence as well.

Galtung (1996) has observed that there are two types of violence, and any positive peace must redress both. Direct violence is the personal suffering of war and physical danger. Structural violence is any form of alienation, repression, or economic dislocation that prevents humans from reaching their full potential. Hunger, poverty, and discrimination are all forms of structural violence that can lead to the outbreak of conflict. Structural violence is not perpetrated by any individual actor, rather it is a product of a certain systemic arrangement. A positive peace will redress these elements of structural violence so that individuals can feel secure in the conduct of their daily lives in a more just international system.

Conflict resolution thus has significant differences from mainstream international relations as an analytical approach (Sandole and Van der Merwe, 1993). International relations primarily focuses on sovereignty, states, great powers, war, foreign policies, and leaders. Conflict resolution, on the other hand, appreciates the role of the individual, the importance of Non-Governmental Organizations (NGOs), and the possibility of track two diplomacy. Conflict resolution looks to the individuals involved in a dispute and asks how each might find a satisfactory compromise that produces a greater instance of positive peace. Conflict resolution has no qualms about opening up the state, looking at interstate as well as intrastate conflicts. From the perspective of settling disputes, there is little difference between a war among states and a war among sub-national groups within a state. All shatter a positive peace. Not being bound by state sovereignty, NGOs can thus play a significant role in dispute resolution. Whereas mainstream international relations often discounts the value of NGOs, they are central in much conflict resolution. Track two diplomacy also moves beyond the traditional notions of foreign policy and diplomacy to embrace individual activism (McDonald and Bendahmane, 1987). Track-two diplomacy involves individuals, operating outside the bounds of any state, intervening on their own accord in a conflict situation. For example, former US president Jimmy

Carter's personal negotiations under the auspices of his Carter Center are high-profile instances of track two diplomacy. On his own, Carter is able to use his prestige and personal style to bypass the stagnant formal policies of governments to create innovative solutions to pressing international disputes. These differences make the study of the settlement of disputes a significantly more normative enterprise than the traditional study of international politics. Traditional modes of analysis treat world events as facts to be studied in an unbiased way. Conflict resolution, however, begins with a normative agenda that peace—a robust positive peace—is a normatively preferable state of affairs.

This activist, normative focus has made negotiation and mediation a central subject for the study of dispute resolution. Both bring the knowledge of the field to practical use in settling disputes. While related, negotiation and mediation have a crucial difference. Negotiations are conducted by the parties to a dispute. They directly engage each other in an attempt to reach a satisfactory settlement. Mediation, on the other hand, involves the intervention of a third party to facilitate negotiations. Thus, mediation involves negotiation, but negotiations do not necessarily require a mediator. Each will be addressed in turn.

NEGOTIATIONS

Negotiations are a strategic dialogue between actors to resolve a situation. Negotiations could determine the allocation of some sort of benefit, a legal standing, a border, economic terms of trade, or any of a whole host of issues. The common threat among negotiations is the strategic bargaining that each side pursues with the other in an attempt to reach a mutually agreeable solution. The study of negotiations is less a theory than it is an analysis of strategy and tactics. In keeping with the practical nature of conflict resolution, studies of negotiations are designed to help negotiators improve their abilities to determine, reach, and implement the best possible settlement they can achieve.

Negotiations often occur in stages. One of the first stages is the pre-negotiation phase, before the parties even begin to discuss a situation (Stein, 1989). Prior to a negotiation, each side prepares what it is willing to compromise and what it will not. These initial conditions often are not conducive to the successful completion of negotiations—if each side comes in unwilling to compromise, believing it has the upper hand, no settlement is likely. Thus, it is important to identify periods of "ripeness," moments when a situation is ripe for a negotiated settlement
(Haass, 1990). The notion of ripeness recognizes that negotiations cannot solve everything. At times, it might be necessary for parties to continue to struggle violently to reach a moment of ripeness. This is a difficult realization for conflict resolution, with its preference for peace and non-violent solutions to conflict. Yet, there are times when one or more sides to a conflict may see continued conflict in their interest, and such situations are not ripe for negotiations.

Once parties enter a negotiation, they enter a situation of strategic bargaining. Negotiations are strategic situations because each side's move depends on the other's choices. All sides make use of some sort of strategy to navigate these interdependent decisions. Schelling's (1980) significant contribution to the study of negotiations was to import game theory into the analysis of the strategic bargaining that occurs in a negotiation. Viewing negotiations as an iterated game, each side must make a credible commitment to convince the other side of its intentions. Thus, through overt or tacit communication, each side binds itself to its commitments, narrowing the scope of potential outcomes until the commitments converge on a solution to the game.

Other approaches to negotiation focus more on the particular strategies negotiators might employ to turn a negotiation in their direction. Many advocate trust-building activities to build ties between the two parties (Zartman and Berman, 1982). Trust allows each side greater leeway in articulating options and boundaries of a settlement. One side may be more willing to give on a certain point if it trusts the intentions of the other side. A particularly influential approach to negotiations urges emphasizes the cooperative, not the competitive nature of a negotiation. A "win-win" approach to negotiations calls for each side to look for the positive outcomes of a negotiation and demands that each party give the other minor victories in order to secure its own. It may be necessary for one or both sides to reevaluate and restructure their interests, but doing so in a way that produces maximum overlap leads to a solution amenable to both (Fisher and Ury, 1983).

When examining the stages of a negotiation, it has become apparent that, especially in international negotiations, several stages occur simultaneously. Most negotiators are engaged in "two-level games" in any negotiation (Evans et al, 1993). The two levels of the game refer to the domestic and international contexts in which a leader must operate. In treaty negotiations, for example, a leader is, in effect, engaged in two simultaneous negotiations on the same issue. At the domestic level, a leader must negotiate within the government on the goals and limits of any outcome. At the international level, the leader must then negotiate the actual treaty. Then again, the leader must sell the agreement to a frequently dissatisfied domestic constituency. As the fulcrum between the two levels, the leader must find a win-set that allows for a solution to the two levels of the negotiation in order to reach a practical solution.

The study of negotiations has produced a myriad of guides, all instructions on the "art of negotiations" in all facets of life. Nevertheless, at the international level, the art of negotiation is studied and practiced to produce non-violent solutions to pressing international problems.

MEDIATION

Direct negotiations between aggrieved parties are difficult even in the most structured of environments. In the highly fluid and unstructured international arena, direct negotiations between groups in conflict are rare and difficult. More frequently, negotiations require the intervention of a third party to mediate.

There are many types of mediation, ranging from the passive to the highly active (Bercovitch, 1996). International negotiations may need only a facilitator to offer "good offices" by passing messages and offering a neutral site for discussions. This type of mediation usually offers technical assistance only, but in doing so, overcomes the interference or bias imposed by location as well as the tension of a direct encounter. Good offices allow the parties to focus on the substantive issues while the mediator handles the technical details of the negotiation process.

Frequently, though, good offices are not enough, and active mediation is required if a negotiation is to reach a settlement

(Crocker et al, 1999). In this case, the mediator becomes an active party to the negotiations, suggesting solutions, pressuring the parties, and, in some cases, serving as a guarantor of the results. In this case, the mediator can restructure the parties' interests and preferences to produce a win-win solution (Fisher and Ury, 1983).

In interstate conflicts, an active mediator is often needed to push negotiations to a conclusion. The presence of the mediator changes the dynamics of the negotiation by offering incentives and pressures that the parties are unable to place upon themselves. For example, the conflict in Bosnia was only resolved after the United States asserted an active role in the mediation process. The US was able to pressure the parties to come to the table through NATO bombing. The US then hosted the talks in Dayton, and proposed many of the solutions in the final agreement. During the Dayton talks, US mediators pressured, cajoled, and promised in order to find an agreeable solution that all parties could sign. Part of the promise was the presence of the IFOR and SFOR peacekeeping troops to ensure the terms of the agreement. The Bosnians, Serbs, and Croats could have provided little of this on their own, but with the active mediation of the United States, they were able to reach a negotiated settlement to their extremely violent conflict.

The UN is perhaps the most active mediator in international conflicts, with the Secretary General offering good offices and special representatives to a wide variety of international conflicts. States also play important roles as mediators—the US in the former Yugoslavia and the Middle East, Norway in Sri Lanka, Costa Rica in Central America. Traditional approaches to power politics discount the important role that these mediators can play in reaching and implementing negotiated solutions to conflicts.

Yet many of the most pressing conflicts today are intrastate conflicts, and they are frequently mediated by individuals and NGOs as much as states and international organizations. Mainstream theories, with their predominant focus on states, have little to contribute to the growing number of civil wars and complex emergencies that occur within the borders of weak and failing states. In this context, the grassroots mediation of an NGO or prominent individual is often more appropriate than state intervention because of the complexity of the situation and the failure of traditional diplomacy (Bercovitch, 1996).

NGOs that mediate in complex humanitarian emergencies and intrastate conflict bring with them a goal of establishing a positive peace. Frequently, NGOs will pool their expertise in economic development, democratization, and humanitarian aid along with their conflict resolution skills to facilitate non-violent ends to conflicts. Conflict resolution offers a more holistic approach to mediation than traditional diplomacy and power politics, making mediation by non-state actors who espouse conflict resolution often highly productive. Moreover, NGOs and individuals are free of the problems and interests that might hamper states who act as mediators. States have histories, including colonial legacies or cold war rivalries, that might prejudice intervention. States also have multiple interests in other areas, such as economic access or other allies that could interfere with mediation. Non-governmental actors often have much narrower agendas that focus on peace and development, avoiding the potential problems of states. Many NGOs, such as the Red Cross or Doctors Without Borders, bring important technical expertise that states lack.

Intervention and mediation in an attempt to solve a conflict is not always successful and not without its flaws (Zartman and Berman, 1982). In some cases, outside intervention in the name of mediation can be harmful. There is no requirement that mediators are neutral parties, and given the increasing interconnectedness of world politics, it is impossible for any actor to be completely neutral and free of any sort of conflict of interest. Mediators that are perceived as overly biased or involved can become parties to the dispute by attempting to impose a solution rather than constructive resolvers of conflict. Moreover, any solution that appears imposed by a heavy-handed mediator could provoke further conflict later. Early in the development of the idea of international conflict resolution, it was assumed that humanitarian aid could be neutral, with no effect on the outcome of a conflict. Today's complex emergencies and civil wars, however, distort that view. Humanitarian assistance can free up internal resources to continue the conflict. Parties can use the temporary cessation in hostilities brought by a mediator to rearm and reorganize their forces. Mediation can also legitimize unsavory rebel groups or governments by recognizing their place at the negotiating table. When mediators attempt to intervene in a conflict not ripe for solution, their efforts may fail. Unfortunately, further violence may lead to ripeness, and premature mediation might prevent the conflict from reaching an appropriate stage of ripeness, ultimately and unintentionally prolonging the conflict instead of resolving it.

PEACE, JUSTICE, AND NON-VIOLENCE

Conflict resolution brings a normative approach to international relations that holds peace, justice, and non-violence as preferable to conflict and power politics. It views realism and liberalism as moral choices and ideologies, not simply scientific approaches to the study of world politics. As such, true conflict resolution is designed to bring about a positive peace which necessarily must end in agreements with structural and cultural change (Bermant et al, 1978). This is in fact a tall order for the practice of conflict resolution, but one enacted through the notion of justice in any negotiated settlement.

While there are a variety of ways to view and evaluate justice, adding this moral dimension to a settlement imposes increased difficulty in the process of reaching negotiated settlements. Negotiations are designed to produce outcomes satisfactory to both parties, and anything agreeable is fair game. Justice, on the other hand, involves an externally imposed standard that frequently favors the interests of one party over another. For example, in both Bosnia and Kosovo, the US negotiated with Slobodon Milosevic, even though Milosevic was branded a war criminal for his role in mass killings. The state interest of a negotiated settlement required a negotiating partner capable of ending the conflict—Milosevic. Justice, however, demanded that Milosevic answer for his war crimes. In practice, the US found it very difficult to bridge these two positions, and in the end preferred to cut a deal with Milosevic rather than pursue justice. Milosevic was brought before an international war crimes tribunal only after his defeat by a domestic opposition. In many cases, conflict resolution practitioners have attempted to bring an element of justice to the settlement of disputes. War crimes tribunals are but one example.

Conflict resolution scholars and practitioners have also explored non-violent means to enact political change. Non-violent intervention, mediation, and protest are difficult practically, but offer a moral authority unmatched in international politics. The celebrated efforts of Gandhi and King relied on a moral case to affect societal change. Non-violent resistance to political conflict forces a society to confront an issue more than violence would. It creates divisions within a society because it makes it more difficult for a leadership and authority structure to justify its actions to its society. The strategy of non-violence relies on the classic observation that all forms of governance depend on consent. As Weber (1978) long ago noted, all forms of political domination ultimately require the consent and cooperation of the governed, which is achieved through legitimacy. Non-violent resistance offers a direct challenge to this legitimacy. The tactic of civil disobedience throws the legitimacy of the leadership into question and forces increasingly more difficult justifications to repress the non-violent uprising. While the approach requires a willingness to endure repression, few open societies can withstand the moral dilemma inherent in attacking peaceful, non-threatening protesters. As a means to change, non-violent resistance is most linked to justice in both means and end results.

CONCLUSION

Mainstream international relations is more concerned with the outbreak of wars than their resolution. A conflict-resolution perspective, however, examines the ways in which actors resolve disputes. With most conflicts ending short of war, and most wars ending short of total victory for one side, negotiation remains the preeminent path to dispute resolution. A conflict-resolution approach reveals the art of negotiation as well as mediation as a vehicle to settle disputes. This approach involves a broader consideration of justice and positive peace, with the normative goal of non-violent and just solutions to pressing world problems to the betterment of all.

BIBLIOGRAPHY

Bercovitch, Jacob. 1996. Resolving International Conflicts: The Theory and Practice of Mediation. Boulder: Lynne Rienner.

Bermant, Gordon, Herbert Kelman, Donald Warwick. 1978. The Ethics of Social Intervention. Washington DC: Hemisphere Publishing Corporation.

Crocker, Chester, Fen Osler Hampson and Pamela Aall. 1999. Herding Cats: The Management of Complex International Mediation. Washington DC: USIP Press.

Evans, Peter, Harold Jacobson, and Robert Putnam. 1993. Double-edged Diplomacy: International Bargaining and Domestic Politics. Berkeley: University of California Press.

Fisher, Roger and William Ury. 1983. Getting to Yes. New York: Penguin.

Galtung, Johan. 1996. Peace by Peaceful Means: Peace and Conflict, Development and Civilization. Thousand Oaks, CA: Sage.

Haass, Richard. 1990. Conflicts Unending: The United States and Regional Disputes. New Haven: Yale University Press.

McDonald, Jr., John and Diane Bendahmane. 1987. Conflict Resolution: Track Two Diplomacy. Washington, DC: Center for the Study of Foreign Affairs.

Rapoport, Anatol. 1992. Peace: An Idea Whose Time Has Come. Ann Arbor: University of Michigan Press.

Sandole, Dennis and Hugo Van der Merwe. 1993. Conflict Resolution: Theory and Practice. New York: St. Martins.

Schelling, Thomas. 1980. The Strategy of Conflict. Cambridge: Harvard University Press.

Stein, Janice Gross. 1989. Getting to the Table, the Process of International Prenegotiation. Baltimore: Johns Hopkins.

Weber, Max. 1978. Economy and Society. Berkeley: University of California Press.

Zartman, I. William and Maureen Berman. 1982. The Practical Negotiator. New Haven: Yale University Press.

XI
DIPLOMACY AND
INTERNATIONAL LAW

Diplomacy is the everyday language of international relations. It is the way in which states interact, the way in which states send signals to each other. Threats, alliances, sanctions, coalitions, and treaties are all the products of diplomacy. Yet diplomacy is more than just the representatives of various states engaging in idle conversation, for such conversations ultimately have little meaning in international politics. Diplomacy gets its stature, meaning, and effectiveness through its relationship to international law. By turning the talk of diplomacy into international law, states are able to develop a body of rules by which to conduct everyday interactions. Thus, to understand diplomacy, it is essential to understand international law (Byers, 2000).

International law forms the basic rules of the game of international politics. Thus, international law has two important functions. First, it constitutes the game, establishing what is and is not within the realm of international relations. Diplomats rely on international law to know what is possible within the game of international relations. Second, it regulates the game, determining the sanctions, rewards, procedures of diplomacy. It tells diplomats how to conduct their business. These two functions allow international law to create and regulate international diplomacy. International law does not determine diplomatic outcomes, rather it facilitates possibilities. It creates a realm of possible, potential, and legal actions. It is left to the diplomats and negotiators to find the best arrangements to fit their particular situation and needs.

DEFINING INTERNATIONAL LAW

The Permanent Court of International Justice decided in the now famous *Lotus* case in 1927 that "international law governs relations between independent states." Others have defined international law as "a body of rules and principles of action that are binding upon civilized states in their relations with one another" (Brierly, 1963). International law consists of internationally recognized rules covering relations between states. In short, it creates the rules of diplomacy.

There are two varieties of international law. There is private international law, generally governing transactions, and public international law, generally setting the contexts and or guidelines for interaction. Before World War two, international law was predominantly a state-centered framework. It consisted almost exclusively of agreements between states about the conduct of international affairs. Developments following World War two have made international law less state-centered and more norm-focused. International law now covers not just state-to-state relations, but the way in which states might treat civilians, commercial transactions, how people relate to the environment, non-governmental organizations, and much more.

The principal distinction between international law and domestic lies in the less-complicated relationship between violation and punishment in domestic systems. In a domestic context, the sovereign government has the authority to enforce the law. The state can punish violations of the law as the system dictates. On the international level, the sovereignty problematic makes this impossible. The modern system of sovereignty grants each sovereign absolute authority to regulate and enforce behavior within its own territory. Yet, all sovereigns are equal in their relations with each other. Thus, there is no way for any actor to enforce international law. There is a paradox between the doctrine of absolute sovereignty and the sanctity of international law, for each forecloses on the possibility of the other. For example, the government of China's actions in response to the student demonstrations at Tiananmen Square in 1989 stood in violation of elements of international human rights laws and treaties to which China was a signatory. Yet, as the sovereign government, China has the sole legitimate right to enforce its own domestic laws within its own territory. Such actions clearly transgress international standards, yet there is no international legal authority to conclusively punish these types of violations. Yet, in the day-to-day practice of diplomacy, both international law and sovereignty coexist in an uneasy fashion.

Writing in the 1860s, philosopher John Austin defined law as "a command from a sovereign" (1996). This definition would suggest that on the international stage, *i.e.* in the absence of a "sovereign," nothing describable as "law" could exist. But many writers argue that even a prominent violation of a rule generally considered part of "international law" does not mean that international law doesn't really exist. As Louis Henkin has observed, "almost all nations observe almost all principles of international law and almost all of their obligations [under it] almost all the time" (1968). Such a conclusion is perhaps unexpected, given the troublesome relationship between sovereignty and international law.

International law is distinguished by its explicit acceptance of multiple sources. Unlike domestic laws that come from one governing body, international law can emerge from any number of sources. The governing statutes of the Permanent Court of International Justice and the International Court of Justice state that in order of precedence, judges will apply international law in the following order, from "hardest" to "softest."

The "hardest" and most definitive source of international law are treaties—signed agreements between states (Reuter, 1992). Treaties are the acts of sovereigns—if sovereigns can agree to a treaty, they are agreeing to relate to each other in a certain way and conduct themselves accordingly. The fundamental axiom of international law is *pacta sunt servanda*, Latin for "one must comply with treaties." As a result, treaties are the hardest form of international law.

The second hardest form of international law is customary practice. That is to say, if a number of state have been doing things a certain way for a period of time, that customary practice has standing as international law. The third level is "Recognized General Principles of Law," which are inferred from rules adopted by a broad variety of states. If a number of states have similar laws governing conduct in a certain area, those laws can be inferred to create an international legal obligation of conduct. Next, judicial decisions by other international legal bodies can contribute to international law. Finally, the softest form of international law is the legal writings of judges and scholars. These legal writings allow new ideas, such as human rights, to enter a legal debate without having become previously codified in a custom or treaty.

For all of international law, state practice plays a significant role. That is to say, the day-to-day conduct of states in their interactions with each other—diplomacy—not only creates international law, but gives it life and meaning. This crucial relationship between law and diplomacy is reflected in the United Nations, a nexus for both international diplomacy and international law. By treaty—the UN charter—UN Security Council Resolutions have force as International Law. Security Council resolutions are binding and enforceable. Thus, there is a significant amount of diplomacy surrounding the security council—both in its membership and the text and voting of its resolutions. By the terms of a prior agreement between all member states—the charter—and as agreements between the member states of the council, resolutions are legally binding on all UN members. They are hard law and are the product of hard diplomacy.

General Assembly resolutions, by contrast, are not hard international law. Such resolutions reflect international opinion, are the products of diplomacy, but are neither binding nor determinant of state practice. As such, there is a different degree and type of diplomacy surrounding the General Assembly. Resolutions passed by the general assembly, given its universality and equality, have some legitimacy as a reflection of world opinion, but that legitimacy is useful only in the practice of diplomacy on those issues. Certain "Important Questions" as defined by the UN Charter—mainly involving the GA's role in overseeing the management of the UN, including its budget and membership on other councils—have a substantial degree of legitimacy, but again, this is due to their standing in an existing treaty, the UN charter.

WHY HAVE INTERNATIONAL LAW?

If the issue of sovereignty makes international law difficult to produce and ultimately unenforceable, what purpose does it serve? There are numerous examples of states flouting international law, including treaties to which that state is a party, to pursue a domestic agenda. For example, in 1999, in the United States, the state of Virginia convicted Paraguayan National Angel Breard of murder and sentenced him to death. The crucial piece of evidence against Breard was a statement he made to police before he could speak to a consular representative of the Paraguayan embassy. Moreover, the US authorities never notified the Paraguayan government that they had tried and sentenced one of their citizens. However, under international law, the Vienna Convention on Consular Relations (1963), all states have a duty to allow foreign nationals to speak to a consular official from their embassy before speaking to anyone else, including the police. The US Secretary of State appealed to the Governor of Virginia to stay the execution pending an appeal of the case based on the provisions of international law. Instead, Virginia executed Breard, pursuing a domestic policy at the expense of an international one. Sovereignty clearly allows the United States to administer its own laws as it sees fit, and yet, the United States violated a treaty it had signed. What good is international law if there is no way to force states to abide by its terms, terms that they have set through diplomacy?

Rarely does such an event happen. As mentioned above, most states obey most international law most of the time. It underpins the practice of diplomacy. Indeed, there is substantial international law on the conduct of diplomacy and status of diplomats to make diplomacy possible. Using this legal framework, diplomats are then able to go about the business of day-to-day state interaction in practice. International law is usually in a state's interest. States sign treaties that they deem favorable, or at a minimum, acceptable. Law protects small states that are not powerful enough to have major armies of their own by giving them rights as sovereigns. It allows powerful states to not use their power all the time. In short, it allows states to get along on a day-to-day basis without having to fight about everything. It provides a framework for diplomacy, even in the most difficult of areas. For example, in 1988, Pan Am flight 103 exploded in mid-air over Lockerbie, Scotland. The United States accused two Libyan agents of planting the bomb. After years of diplomacy, the two countries have relied on international law to settle the dispute. They resolved the situation by placing the two suspects on trial by Scottish judges under Scottish law in a former American Air Force Base in the Netherlands. The legal framework and diplomatic practice resolved this very difficult issue between two states that, previously, could not agree on anything.

International law also serves as a way to ensure reciprocity among states. Many states obey the fundamentals of international law in their diplomacy because they expect other states to reciprocate in kind. This codified reciprocity adds a tremendous amount of stability to what could otherwise be a turbulent international environment. States then don't have to spend time or energy worrying about what should be a trivial and routine matter because they can count on reciprocity from other states.

Much international law and diplomacy are effective because they solves what would otherwise become massive coordination problems. Much commercial law exists to avoid endless diplomacy. The standards and procedures established by law allow routine conduct to proceed without having to renegotiate standards and procedures each and every time. For example, international telephone calls, postal deliveries, air travel, and trade occur so much and so often and in such volume that it is impossible to negotiate each and every instance. So, there is law about how to deliver mail between states, even in times of war. There is law about how planes can fly across borders and oceans and not crash into each other. In each case, international law produced by diplomacy coordinates routine international activity.

Finally, states use international law as a tool in communicating with each other. It is a vital element of diplomacy. When a state embarks on a controversial path, it will frequently justify the new policy by offering reasons from international law. If a country can say that its actions are "legal," then others are more willing accept them. Calling state action "illegal" is used as a prelude and justification for further action.

The law and diplomacy surrounding the recent war in Kosovo are illustrative. Concerned about the province of Kosovo, the United States attempted to bring the government of Yugoslavia and representatives of the Kosovars together to sign a treaty. This bit of diplomacy was aimed at producing international law—diplomacy to produce an agreement about the status of Kosovo and a treaty to formalize it in routine practice. When this diplomacy failed, the UN took up the matter. It was unable to resolve the issue. Concerned for the plight of the Kosovars, the US initiated a military campaign of bombing Yugoslavia. The US justified its decision with the Genocide Convention, which makes Genocide a crime under international law. That communicated the intent of the US campaign. Moreover, the military action came under the auspices of NATO, a multilateral military alliance. The Yugoslav government cited international law and sovereignty in protest. It claimed that, under the sovereignty provisions of the UN charter, it and it alone had the right to administer the domestic governance of its territory absent outside interference. The United States, on the other hand, cited the provisions of the Genocide Convention and other articles in the UN charter that allow regional organizations such as NATO to enforce treaties such as the Genocide Convention. In this case, international law offered a range of possibilities. It enabled the US to conduct a war over Kosovo, and provided a justification for that war. It also offered a defense for Yugoslavia. Neither side was clear-cut, and it was only through the practice of politics—diplomacy—at the international level, that states found a resolution to this crisis.

International law and diplomacy exist hand in hand because each is necessary for the existence of the other. This holds true in nearly all facets of international relations. It is most notable in issues of peace and security. The UN charter and UN Security council resolutions establish law on how states must respond to international disputes and aggression. Yet there is also a significant body of law on how to conduct diplomacy and even war. These laws rely heavily on reciprocity, for sovereignty makes it possible for any state to breach any aspect of international law. Yet, in general, states treat prisoners of war humanely, refrain from using weapons of mass destruction and avoid land mines, not just because it is international law, but because they expect other states to respond in kind. Similar provisions exist for the international environment, as well as commercial areas. Law and diplomacy work hand in hand to produce the world politics that we know today.

One of the most substantial trends in international law is the beginning of a move toward enforcement at an international level. As noted before, sovereignty makes this difficult, but slowly, international law and diplomacy have been able to trump sovereignty. The UN Security Council has the ability to call upon member states to enforce its resolutions and provisions of international law. Most dramatically this has happened with Iraq in 1991. Yet is the establishment of international criminal courts that mark the most dramatic changes to international law. The security council set up two independent and ad hoc International Criminal Tribunals to try individuals for crimes in the former Yugoslavia and Rwanda. The pending Rome Treaty, establishing a permanent International Criminal Court, would make such a judicial body permanent.

These courts are quite controversial because they conflict with the fundamental premise of international law and diplomacy—sovereignty. The power of the sovereign to act with impunity at home and abroad remains the fundamental issue of international diplomacy and the ultimate foil to effective international law. International law works as an effective tool of diplomacy, but only as much as the sovereign states allow it. The idea of sovereignty is so deeply engrained as the constitutive rule of the international system that it is unlikely that law will ever trump diplomacy, and yet the very practice of diplomacy depends on the existence of international law. This fundamental tension, between law and diplomacy, continues to define and propel international politics.

BIBLIOGRAPHY

Austin, John. 1996. *Lectures on Jurisprudence*. Bristol: Thoemmes Press.

Brierly, James Leslie. 1963. *The Law of Nations: An Introduction to the International Law of Peace*, 6th edition. Oxford: Clarendon Press.

Byers, Michael. 2000. *The Role of Law in International Politics*. Oxford: Oxford University Press.

Henkin, Louis. 1968. *How Nations Behave: Law and Foreign Policy*. New York: The Council on Foreign Relations.

Reuter, Paul. 1992. *Introduction to the Law of Treaties*. London: Pinter.

XII
COLONIZATION AND IMPERIALISM

It is impossible in a single discussion to deal with the subject of imperialism and colonialism, even if it is tied to a particular geographical location and time. This discussion will very broadly address modern European colonization on the continent of Africa. Short case studies will be used to elaborate a particular strategy of colonization. Europeans were by no means the only group to engage in the conquest and political control of peoples on the continent of Africa. African Arabs and other groups of Africans also politically and economically dominated other groups on the continent and their land. However, the scope, force, and length of foreign occupation were much less than that of the colonizing powers of Europe who dominated African polities in the nineteenth and twentieth centuries.

Imperialism developed as a term after 1870 to describe a system of organized colonial trade and organized colonial rule. V. I. Lenin theorized that the wheels of capitalism in Europe were oiled by profits earned from investments in colonies. Lenin argued that the scarcity of "unclaimed" land would be the only limitation to European imperialism. After that point, imperialist expansion could occur only at the expense of other imperialist states, leading to inter-imperialist competition and war.

Prior to the 1840s, Europeans had traded with Africans but their activities were limited to the outskirts of the continent in the coastal regions. European powers, including Portugal, Spain,

England, Holland, France, Denmark, Sweden and Germany, engaged in trade in gold, pepper, spices, ivory, and human beings, after plantation economy based on slave labor developed in the Caribbean and the United States. From 1840's onwards, there was a marked increase in European activities in Africa. Explorers went to Africa intending to map the geographical area and to "open up" Africa to Europe. By 1870, this effort had gained such momentum that diplomatic initiatives were required in order to avoid conflicts in the competition for land and control.

In 1885 at the Berlin Conference, representatives from France, Britain, Portugal, Germany, Belgium, Spain and Italy met to outline the rules of the "Scramble for Africa." At this conference they decided how they were going to divide up Africa. By 1900, the entire continent had been mapped out and laid clear. The Berlin Conference, held in Europe, adjudicated the borders of European colonies on the continent of Africa. European imperialists used guns and goods to make deals with locals that were willing to help them achieve their colonial goals. With the formation of boundaries, the European countries went in and established bureaucracies, administrations, military bases and organizations as well as the infrastructure (roads, buildings, schools) that became part of colonial rule. From 1885 to 1960, there was colonial rule in most of Africa. With the exception of Liberia, at one time or another, almost all countries on the continent of Africa have been under European rule.

Britain, France, Belgium and Portugal were the largest colonial powers after 1900. France was dominant in North, West and Central Africa. French possessions in Africa included present-day Equatorial Guinea, part of Somaliland, Guinea, Chad,

Algeria, Morocco, Tunisia, Mauritania, Senegal, Guinea, Mali, Niger, Ivory Coast, Burkina Faso, Benin, and Madagascar. Britain had a strong presence in Southern and East Africa. Britain controlled Sudan, Kenya, Uganda, part of Somaliland, Egypt, The Gambia, Sierra Leone, Ghana, Nigeria, Zanzibar, South Africa, and present-day Zimbabwe. Belgium dominated much of Central Africa, as it possessed the Congo. Portugal's influence was also in the southern region. Portugal held Angola, Mozambique, Sao Tome and Principe, and the Cape Verde Islands. Germany held Togo, Cameroon, Rwanda, Tanganyika, and Namibia. Shortly after the First World War, Germany lost all possessions on the continent. Italy held Libya, part of Somaliland, and Eritrea. Spain held the Sahara Province, Rio Muni, Fernando Po, Annobon, and the smaller territories of Ceuta, Melilla, and Ifni.

Why did the scramble for Africa happen? There are two main arguments. First, there is the economic argument that Europe needed a place to put capital, and raw materials to serve as direct inputs to industry. In addition to capital and inputs, industrial capitalists in Europe needed markets to sell their manufactured goods. So capitalism expanded to other regions of the world. The concept of imperialism refers to a particular stage of development of the capitalist economy. Imperialism is understood as an economic system of external investment and external control of markets and sources of raw materials.

The second prominent argument used to explain the "Scramble for Africa" is that European countries went in after 1870 largely because of strategic competition and rivalry. They saw other European powers going in and considered the possible threats to their security if the balance of power in Europe was disrupted. King Leopold's expansion into central Africa is often used to support this point. Britain, France and Portugal were already on the continent. Hence, Belgium felt compelled to build their resources through the acquisition of colonies. Belgium was a late mover in the political game. Like most European powers, the Belgians started on the coast and expanded inward to eventually claim a vast territory in central Africa. According to this approach, strategic competition fueled or motivated imperialism in Africa. In this view, colonialism is an inevitable consequence of great power politics.

However, there are other explanations for Europe's preoccupation with Africa. For example, some missionaries were convinced that the best way to squelch the practice of slavery and to improve life on the continent was through the conversion of its inhabitants to Christianity. Although economic gain was the dominant motive, philanthropy and moral enrichment also constituted important strands in colonial policies. After slavery was internationally outlawed, the whole basis of European trading activities and presence in Africa took on a new character. Africa became a source of raw materials for the rapidly expanding industries of Western Europe. The development of this new kind of trade called for both European investments of capital and effective political control on the continent.

COLONIALISM IN AFRICA

Strategies of colonial rule ranged from ensuring control through the use of violence to divide-and-rule and strategic alliances with local groups. Like with the slave trade, colonial rule was made possible through collaboration with members of various sectors of African societies. The values of a particular

European country were generally reflected in its relationship with their colonies. As such, European powers followed different colonial policies. The rest of this paper will discuss two types of colonial administration perform by two great imperial powers, Great Britain and France.

BRITISH COLONIAL POLICY: INDIRECT RULE

Wherever possible in their African territories, Britain tried to rule through existing and traditional authorities. They retained certain elements of indigenous institutions and used them to develop their own colonial administration. Local authority figures were subject to the approval of British government officials. British government officials adopted the role of adviser to indigenous political leaders. The British authorities guided the native rulers in what they perceived as their gradual development process from a traditional, barbaric system of governance to a political system of modern local government. It was left up to each individual colony to determine the pace of its own evolution, depending on social and economic resources and the particular administrator in charge of affairs. The relationship between the British colonial official and the native leader was cooperative. However, it was also inherently an asymmetric power relationship as the British administrator managed it. England required that the inhabitants of the colonies pledged their allegiance to the British government rather than the local. Colonial subjects were forced to pay taxes to Britain, serve in the British army, and give their land over to the British.

One of Britain's most notable colonial administrators, Lord Lugard, outlined the principles of indirect rule in his influential book *The Dual Mandate in Tropical Africa*. Lugard argued that "decentralization" and "continuity" are central administrative principles. The colonial government must delegate powers to local district officers. This was necessary in order to ensure the economic and moral advancement of the natives. Continuity was achieved through the appointment of "primitive peoples" at all administrative levels. The practice of including natives in the colonial government served another goal as well. It ensured British rule by contributing to stability of the colony. In the interest of maintaining law and order, Lugard argued that a delicate balance between tradition and modernity must be maintained.

Lugard eventually published a guide for British administrative officials. In the monograph, he emphasized the importance of acknowledging and not destroying authority networks already in place. British officials were to rule through native authorities. By using indigenous institutions and authorities, British officials were to ensure stability through keeping the structures that the peoples were familiar with, while laying the groundwork for a more modern society. Indirect rule was based on the assumption that British colonial territories were possessions held only until their inhabitants were sufficiently trained in modern practices and advanced in managing modern institutions. Only after achieving this level of sophistication could the colonial inhabitants take on the responsibility of governing themselves. However, it was not conceptualized as a fast approaching reality.

FRENCH COLONIAL POLICY: DIRECT RULE AND ASSIMILATION

French colonial policy was based on two principles, direct rule and assimilation. Committed to the Roman tradition of empire, the French felt a duty to extend the wealth of their civilization to the primitive inhabitants of their colonies. The French colonial theory of 'mission civilatrice' required a homogeneous, rational administrative policy for all of their African empire. The French pursued this policy, largely ignoring existing indigenous social and political institutions. French colonies were made constitutional and administratively equal parts of continental France. In the French colonial administration, power was unevenly distributed. All authority was centralized in Paris, and filtered down to the local governors and assemblies.

After demonstrating a mastery of French civilization, colonial inhabitants could then be awarded with French citizenship. The principle of assimilation is rooted in the notion that through education and other forms of social engineering, differences between people could be eliminated. Political assimilation was the confluence of two seemingly contradictory beliefs: the belief in equality among men and the belief that French race was superior. Direct rule was necessary to oversee the process of civilizing the Africans towards eventual assimilation. However, the assimilation was never fully enacted in French colonial policy. A very small number of the inhabitants were ever accorded citizenship. Hence, the vast majority of the inhabitants of French colonies had the inferior status of 'sujet' (subject people), which mean they were subject to the justice adjudicated by the colonial administration and forced labor practices. Two central features of the French colonial system were the imposition of a poll tax and forced labor on all of the adult population without the status of full French citizenship.

THE DE-COLONIZATION PROCESS

World War II and the post-war period brought changes in both the French and British colonial policies. Forced labor and the status of 'sujet' as well as other restrictive laws were abolished, and the colonies were later given increased control over their own affairs. By the end of the Second World War, British colonial policy stated that Britain had the responsibility of ensuring economic and social advancement in the colonies in order to provide the basis for self-rule. Why this change in policy? The Second World War had taken a serious economic and psychological toll on the colonial powers. European states' power dramatically declined on account of losses incurred during World War II. State officials were more concerned with the rebuilding their nation. Furthermore, the domestic politics of the colonial powers saw the rise of political parties in favor of granting the colonies their independence.

Another reason for this change in policy was the emergence of the United States and the Soviet Union as superpowers from World War II, with significantly increased economic and political power. Both superpowers were against imperial policies and the maintenance of colonies. War-affected European states were in some way dependent on these superpowers for reconstruction funding and assistance. Changed dynamics at the international level meant that the colonial powers were subject to the demands of the United States and the Soviet Union.

The change in colonial policy was also encouraged by the political leadership of nationalist elites, who lead popular national movements. These national leaders had studied in Europe or the United States and were both intellectually and experientially aware of the contradictions inherent in the colonial situation. While European and North Americans preached the universal equality of all peoples, they practiced the opposite in their foreign occupation of Africa. In addition, during both wars soldiers from the continent of Africa fought side by side with European soldiers. More similarities between the men became apparent in the context of war. This new class of educated and traveled Africans supported anti-colonial nationalist movements.

International social movements also influenced African struggles for liberation. Nationalist movements in India propelled de-colonization in India (1947) which set the stage for British withdrawal from its imperial endeavors. Following British withdrawal, the French pulled out of Vietnam (1954). During this time, the Civil Rights movement in the US was also gaining momentum. These actions were influential factors in Europe's retreat from African territories.

The anti-colonial movements had different outcomes and different patterns of decolonization of Africa. Generally, there were three types of decolonization: elite negotiation, mass mobilization and violence. Elite negotiation happened when a small group of national elites petitioned for independent and scheduled a transfer of rule, *i.e.* Nigeria. Mass mobilization involved mass gatherings and demonstrations, *i.e.* Ghana. In Guinea, civil disobedience and strikes were used to bring Europeans to the table. The last kind of strategy used was armed struggle. However, usually the first two strategies were tried and met with violence from a European colonial power before Africans retaliated with arms.

Gaining independence for some colonies was a painful process. This experience was probably most acute in Algeria, which was a settlement colony and for nearly a century had been administered as virtually a part of France. In 1962, there were about 400,000 French settlers in Algeria who owned most of the territory's farmland. Here, the French never entertained the possibility of eventual self-government for the local populace, and no attempt was made to devise political institutions for such an eventuality. When the population began to agitate seriously for independence in the 50s, white settlers vehemently resisted France's attempts at granting concessions. The white settlers had come to regard the country as their rightful and exclusive possession, and it was only after a long and bitter war (1954-1962) that the Algerians succeeded in wresting their freedom from France.

The European powers also had different styles of engaging with their former colonies. After 1960s, France was actively involved in the political and economic affairs of former French Africa. The French developed a monetary system for all former colonies, which was tied to the French franc. Britain had a more distant relationship with its former colonies. Former British colonies form what is referred to as the Commonwealth, but it is not a tight alliance. It is a diplomatic and consultative organization.

CONCLUSION

Africa endured radical changes in every sphere of life as a result of colonialism. Politically, the decisive change was the creation of new states. Pre-colonial political organization was replaced by bureaucratic military centralized rule. Homogenous societies became part of larger diverse societies, and many different languages were spoken within the borders of a centralized political state. Moreover, the official state languages are those of the former European rulers. An important legacy of colonialism on the continent of Africa is the contentious boundary issue, which was accepted by the national elites upon independence.

The political boundaries established generally do not reflect indigenous racial, tribal, and cultural patterns and are often a source of conflicts. In Nigeria, for example, there are 250-400 ethnic linguistic groups, organized by arbitrary political boundaries that divided members of the same group (Yoruba and Hausa) across at least two or more different states in West Africa. Lastly, following decolonization, African states were integrated into the international states system and subject to international law and diplomacy.

Colonialism also had profound and dramatic changes on the economic life of Africans. The economy was no longer embedded within the social life of the African societies. New notions of property rights and wage labor, trade and commercialization of production needed to be dealt with as most people became integrated in the money economy. Money currency had become the standard medium of exchange, and the use of money was generalized through taxation. The money economy and commodity production had spread into the hinterland, marking a move from self-sufficient rural production to cash commodity. Trade increased agricultural production. The wage laborer became a feature of the society. Property rights also changed. Property was brought and sold by owners. Although not everyone moved to the city and subsistence farming did not halt, there was an integrated money economy, which had not existed before.

Since 1960s, the independent states of Africa have faced the incredible and overwhelming challenge of simultaneous state-building, nation-building and economic development. African countries have faced the difficulties of consolidating centralized public authority and the development of national state institutions that could provide governance. Many African countries have experienced difficulties in forging unified political communities from plural states. The difficulties of managing competition and strife among ethnic communities and promoting common symbols and identities have placed substantial demands upon governments throughout the region. Economic development is another concern for African state leaders. There is a myriad of challenges of growth and structural transformation in low-income agrarian economies. They have to promote rapid growth, reduce poverty, and negotiate economic structural change. The legacy of colonization and imperialism has presented many challenges to the states on the continent of Africa, many of which African leaders are still attempting to overcome today.

BIBLIOGRAPHY

Alexander, Archibald. 1969. *A History of Colonization on the Western Coast of Africa*. New York: Negro Universities Press.

Boyd, W. D. 1962. "The American Colonization Society and the Slave Recaptives of 1860-1861: An Early Example of United States–African Relations." *Journal of Negro History* 17:2.

Buell, Raymond Leslie. 1965. *The Native Problem in Africa, I-II*. London: Frank Cass.

Clendenen, Clarence, Robert Collins and Peter Duignan. 1966. *Americans In Africa 1865-1900*. Stanford: Hoover Institution on War, Revolution, and Peace, Standard University.

Collins, Robert O. et al. 2001. *Problems in African History*. Princeton: Markus Wiener Publishers.

Duignan, Peter and L. H. Gann. 1984. *The United States and Africa: A History*. Cambridge: Cambridge University Press.

Gifford, Prosser and William Roger. 1982. *The Transfer of Power in Africa, Decolonization, 1940-1960*. New Haven: Yale University Press.

Iliffe, John. 1995. *Africans: The History of a Continent*. Cambridge: Cambridge University Press.

Young, Crawford. 1994. *The African Colonial State in Comparative Perspective*. New Haven: Yale University Press.

XIII
INTERNATIONAL
DEVELOPMENT

In 1950, the average per capita income of low-income countries was $164 versus $3,841 for the industrial countries. By 1995, the more industrialized countries had a per capita average of $24,930 versus $430 in the low-income countries (Seligson and Passe-Smith, 1998). Over the past four decades, less affluent states' preoccupation with various development strategies has yielded modest returns, if any. Scholars have examined the development process through different conceptual lenses. The most salient approaches are cultural (modernization) and structural (dependency, neo-Marxist, and World Systems) approaches. Due to the breadth of these discussions, only the most salient aspects of these approaches will be discussed.

After World War II, European capitalists preoccupied with achieving profits, extracting raw materials, and developing new markets in colonized countries, became concerned with transforming the agrarian subsistence societies into modern industrial societies. Scholars presumed that financial and technical assistance would stimulate this process. They reasoned that high levels of economic development and modernization would lead to political development. Political development understood as the establishment of a modern political democracy, including formal and representative institutions. These theorists advocated what became know as modernization theory. Using advanced capitalist states as a model, development was envisioned as a unidirectional, linear path. However, the neat unidirectional and linear path of economic and political progress outlined by modernization theorists was challenged by dependency and world systems theorists as well as scholars such as Barrington Moore and Samuel Huntington. In conclusion, this chapter will address recent critiques of development performed by Arturo Escobar and James Scott, who are sometimes referred to as post-development scholars.

MODERNIZATION THEORY

In his book *The Stages of Economic Growth*, Rustow (1960) theorized the development process by identifying five stages of economic development. The first stage consisted of a traditional society, which is predominantly agricultural. In the second stage the preconditions for development are established. Technological advances and social innovations characterize the second stage. During the third stage, barriers to economic growth disappear. Commercialization, industry, and investment thrive. Development "takes off." In the fourth stage, the economy matures and surplus production is achieved. In the fifth stage, high mass consumerism takes place. There is an economic shift towards producing consumer goods and services. As a result of industrialization, urbanization ensues.

Organski (1965), in his book *Stages of Political Development*, examined the role of government through four stages: 1) primitive national unification 2) industrialization 3) national welfare, and 4) abundance. He defined development in terms of increasing government efficiency in mobilizing human and material resources toward national ends. Apter (1965) claims that modernization is a particular type of development. He identifies two models of modernization: 1) secular-libertarian (or pluralistic systems like the US) 2) sacred collectivity (or mobilizing systems like China under Mao). In an effort to avoid the unidirectional and evolutionary overtones of simplistic stage theory, Black (1966) emphasizes the challenges involved in the shift from traditional to modern practices, the obstacles confronting the consolidation of modern political leadership, and the problems incurred in the creation of an urban and industrial form.

DEVELOPMENT

According to some scholars, the experience of advanced capitalist societies suggested a linear path toward modern development. Weber attempted to understand the nature of modern capitalism in his work. Parsons' interpretation of Weber's informed his systems theory. Parsons' ideal type of traditional and modern societies influenced the mainstream approach to the study of development and modernization and also spawned structural-functionalism. Almond and Coleman (1960), in *The Politics of Developing Areas,* provide a new theoretical approach for comparative politics and development. Structural-functionalism treats certain social functions as inputs to the making of a "developed" society, including interest articulation, interest aggregation, communication, and socialization. Likewise, there are social functions that are understood as outputs of society such as rule making, rule execution, and rule adjudication. Social systems could then be compared according to the existence or absence of institutions that fulfill certain functions. Based on these insights, social systems could be designed to achieve economic goals.

The structural-functionalist paradigm is expanded by Almond and Powell's (1966) *Comparative Politics: A Developmental*

Approach. In their monograph, they postulate three levels of functions performed by all political systems: 1) system capabilities 2) conversion functions, and 3) system maintenance and adaptive functions. Political development involves structural differentiation, cultural secularization, and increased sub-system autonomy as it meets the problems of state-building, nation-building, participation, and distribution. Many critiques were made on the structural-functional approach employed in the numerous books sponsored by the SSRC from 1963 to 1978 (see Tilly, 1975).

Scholars also became concerned with clarifying the term development. What did it mean? What did it entail? Are there any limits to this phenomenon? In *Aspects of Political Development*, Lucian Pye (1966) summarizes the various meanings attributed to the development concept into three categories: 1) increased equality among individuals in relation to the system 2) increased capacity of the system regarding its political environment 3) increased differentiation of institutions and structures within the system.

PROBLEMS WITH MODERNIZATION THEORY

Moore (1966) challenged the notion that modernization was inevitable given a certain set of conditions and the idea that there is only one way for development to happen. In his book *Social Origins of Dictatorship and Democracy*, he performs a comparative analysis of several countries to determine the causal factors that lead to national political outcomes: democracy, fascism, and communism. Moore finds that political outcomes could be predicted by studying the particular way in which social forces interacted through history. His study focuses on socio-economic classes—lord, peasant, and bourgeoisie—and their interrelations over time. According to Moore, a bourgeoisie revolution fosters capitalism and parliamentary democracy. The consequences of the revolution include the elimination of the peasantry, a balance between the crown and the aristocracy, and a dynamic urban commercial sector, all of which set the stage for capitalism and democracy to take root. A weak bourgeoisie and conservative reactionary revolution from above foster fascism. The existence of a strong aristocracy, the exploitation of peasants, and the retention of feudal norms are characteristics of a fascist political system. A peasant revolution from below fosters communism. A communist form of political organization came from great agrarian bureaucracies that destroyed the prevailing social organization of the peasants but failed to make the transition to commercial agriculture.

In his book *Political Order in Changing Societies*, Huntington (1968) rejects the structural-functionalist claim that development was semiautomatic. He points out that political instability often occurs as a result of rapid social change, modernization, and the mobilization of new groups into politics while there is a paucity of efficient and effective institutions. Modernization, understood as social mobilization, economic development, and political modernization, increases conflict between traditional groups and modern ones. Huntington identifies the lag in the development of political institutions as the central problem in all development efforts. Development, according to Huntington, is incredibly difficult. The key to both political and economic development is the successful creation of institutions.

DEPENDENCY AND WORLD SYSTEMS THEORY

Theorists from the dependency school criticize modernization theorists for assuming that underdevelopment was an original stage of traditional society when, in fact, it was a consequence of European imperialism and colonialism. Most modernization theorists ignored both historical conditions and relations between the underdeveloped and developed countries. Underdevelopment was not a natural condition but one that was created by the capitalist international system. Dependency theory is premised on unequal exchange between the core countries of the North and the peripheral South. The economies of the center develop at the expense of the periphery—thus the development of underdevelopment thesis. Frank (1969) argued that an adequate theory of development could not be formulated without attention to the past economic and social history of underdevelopment suffered by the majority of the world's population. Furthermore, the view of dual societies, traditional and modern, is false because the underdevelopment of certain countries is the result of the same process that produced developed countries. These societies are not separate phenomena. Capitalism on a world scale promotes developing metropolises at the expense of under-developing satellites and making them dependent.

Rather than focusing on cultural and social forces in development, the dependency school emphasizes the primacy of structural economic and political factors. It decries the heavy penetration of foreign capital, the unbalanced reliance upon the export of a few primary products, unequal exchange, and the symbiotic relationship of the local elites with external investors. Dependency theorists deny the possibility of piecemeal reforms because it is impossible to develop within the global capitalist system as it disadvantages the so-called Third World. According to some dependency theorists, development theory is another form of imperialism. Inspired by the work of Frank and others, Cardoso and Faletto (1979) in *Dependency and Development in Latin America* argue that capitalism does not promote underdevelopment in all sphere of a society; instead capitalist development can foster dependency. They claim that development in the form of capitalism benefits those tied to international capital, but undermines national interests that are not linked to multinational corporations. This, in turn, creates a schism in the populace and political instability, prompting military intervention and rule.

In his book *The Modern World System*, Wallerstein (1974) built on the work of dependency theorists who called attention to the relationship between a few countries and emphasized a world system of relations. Wallerstein introduces his structural analysis with the assertion that the study of social change should be restricted to the study of changes in structural phenomena since they are most durable. For Wallerstein, the only social system is the world-system, and this is where social change takes place. A geographical division of labor magnifies and legitimizes the ability of some groups within the system to exploit the labor of others. Capitalism is based on the constant absorption of economic loss by political entities, while economic gain is distributed to private hands. To the dependency's core-periphery distinction, Wallerstein adds the semi-periphery. Semi-peripheral areas are a necessary structural element because they deflect pressure from the core. Since the sixteenth century, center countries—many European countries and the United

States—have developed in large part due to colonization and exploitation of periphery and semi-periphery countries. As a result, both political and economic development is impeded in the countries of the periphery and semi-periphery.

PROBLEMS WITH DEPENDENCY AND WORLD SYSTEMS THEORY

Unfortunately, Wallerstein offers only a reductionist neo-Smithian model, which ignores all other factors and concentrates exclusively on market forces. His model is mechanical in that it focuses on core-periphery relations and foregoes the complexity of social relations. Wallerstein does not deal with production and production relations, which is the nitty-gritty of the neo-Marxist paradigm. If one posits that the root problem in North-South relations is imbalance in the world economy, it follows that the solution is to establish balance through the distribution of wealth. The distribution of wealth alone cannot erase the structures of global inequality. As long as the social relations that underpin these structures remain intact, transferring capital and technology into underdeveloped countries would at best be a palliative.

As insightful as structural explanations of underdevelopment are, they tend to be overly deterministic: given certain structures, outcomes follow. Structural causes are so powerful that everything becomes predictable. In contrast to culturalists, structuralists argue that structure is significant and individual actions play a peripheral role, if any. When structuralists consider individuals, they tend to homogenize them. The dependency school fails to draw distinctions within the populace of the core and the periphery. Dependency and the world systems theory fail to account for change. And lastly, if it is the structure of the international economy and external factors that underdeveloped the Third World, how do we account for the remarkable economic performance of the East Asian newly industrializing countries (NICs)?

DEMOCRACY AND DEVELOPMENT

In the 1970s and 1980s, development gets fused into democratization and political culture. Many scholars shifted their focus to democratization because of the failure of structural-functionalism to explain historical outcomes and because of the various critiques of the notion of development and its theoretical claims. Also, the proliferation of newly democratizing countries in the 1970s and 1980s demanded attention. O'Donnell and Schmitter (1986) argue that in the case of newly democratizing countries, political development is seen not simply as a product of modernization and economic development. Instead, they focus on the role that political elites and pacts play in the breakdown, transition, and consolidation of political democracy. Much of the democratization literature that follows adopts this approach and concentrates on the transition and consolidation phases of democratization in their examination of democratic political development (see Huntington (1991), Linz & Stepan (1996), Diamond (1997)).

Some scholars argue that political culture is key to understanding where and why democratic development is successful or not. Putnam (1993) attempts to explain the difference in performance of Italian regional governments. He claims that the key to economic and political development is social capital (norms of trust, cooperation, and reciprocity). If relations among individuals over time are horizontal and pluralistic, social capital will be high. This is needed to build effective democratic institutions. Thus, strong democratic institutions must be built from below. Others, most notably Fukuyama (1995) makes a similar argument. They place an emphasis on trust and social capital as essential for the prospect of developing a democratic order.

POST-DEVELOPMENT CRITIQUES OF "DEVELOPMENT"

In his book *Encountering Development*, Escobar (1995) begins with the question: How did the industrialized nations of Europe and North America come to be seen as the appropriate models for the post-WWII societies of Asia, Africa, and Latin America? How did the post-war discourse on development actually create the so-called Third World? Escobar identifies three axes of the development discourse: the forms of knowledge that refer to it and through which it comes into being, the systems of power that regulate its practice, and the forms of subjectivity fostered by it. These forms of subjectivity are the lenses through which people come to recognize themselves as developed or underdeveloped.

Escobar borrows heavily from Foucault in terms of his conceptions of knowledge, power, and truth. Power enables the production of truth, and in the case of Escobar, this means the construction of poverty and its requisite, socially constructed 'cure': development. Those pushing development claimed that capital, science, and technology were essential for the underdeveloped world if they hoped to follow the path of 'advanced' societies. Yet, the discourse and strategy of development produced massive underdevelopment and impoverishment, and untold exploitation and oppression. The development discourse created an extremely efficient apparatus for producing knowledge about, and exercise of power over, the so-called Third World. Beneath development's emancipatory facade, there sits a project to control and manage the people and environment of the Third World. Escobar is able to investigate the contradictions inherent in development discourse in an attempt to help subjugated knowledges emerge. Like Foucault, he rebuffs grand theory and rather looks to concrete, localized settings as the breeding grounds for resistance.

POST-DEVELOPMENT CRITIQUES OF DEVELOPMENT PRACTITIONERS

In the mid 1990s, Claude Ake, a Nigerian social scientist, asked why despite three decades of preoccupation with development in Africa the economies of most African nations are still stagnating or regressing. For most Africans, incomes are lower than they were two decades ago, health prospects are poorer, malnutrition is widespread, and infrastructures and social institutions are disintegrating. Ake contends that the problem is not that development has failed but it was never really tried in Africa. He maintains that the political leadership in African countries is the greatest impediment to development. In his book *Development and Democracy in Africa* (1996), Ake traces the evolution and failure of development policies, including the International Monetary Fund's stabilization programs that have dominated international efforts. He asserts that the authoritarian structure the African state inherited from colonial rule created a political environment that was hostile to development. Ake emphasizes the importance of local African social and political institutions in building a new paradigm for development based on traditional agricultural techniques and indigenous political practices.

BIBLIOGRAPHY

Ake, Claude. 1996. *Democracy and Development in Africa.* Washington, DC: Brookings Institution.

Almond, Gabriel Abraham and G. Bingham Powell, Jr. 1966. *Comparative Politics: A Developmental Approach.* Boston: Little, Brown.

Almond, Gabriel Abraham and James S. Coleman. 1960. *The Politics of The Developing Areas.* Princeton: Princeton University Press.

Apter, David Ernest. 1965. *The Politics of Modernization.* Chicago: University of Chicago Press.

Cardoso, Fernando Henrique. 1979. *Dependency and Development in Latin America.* Berkeley: University of California Press.

Escobar, Arturo. 1995. *Encountering Development: The Making And Unmaking Of The Third World.* Princeton: Princeton University Press.

Frank, Andre Gunder. 1969. *Capitalism And Underdevelopment In Latin America; Historical Studies Of Chile And Brazil.* New York: Monthly Review Press.

Fukuyama, Francis. 1995. *The Social Virtues And The Creation Of Prosperity.* New York: Free Press.

Huntington, Samuel. 1968. *Political Order In Changing Societies.* New Haven: Yale University Press.

Huntington, Samuel. 1991. *The Third Wave: Democratization in the Late Twentieth Century.* Norman: University of Oklahoma Press.

Linz, Juan and Alfred Stepan. 1996. *Problems of Democratic Transition and Consolidation: Southern Europe, South America, and Post-Communist Europe.* Baltimore: Johns Hopkins University Press.

Moore, Barrington. 1966. *Social Origins Of Dictatorship And Democracy; Lord And Peasant In The Making Of The Modern World.* Boston: Beacon Press.

O'Donnell, Guillermo, Phillipe Schmitter, and Whitehead. 1986. *Transitions from Authoritarian Rule: Tentative Conclusions About Uncertain Democracies.* Baltimore: Johns Hopkins University Press.

Organski, A. F. K. 1965. *The Stages of Political Development.* New York: Knopf.

Putnam, Robert. 1993. *Making Democracy Work: Civic Traditions in Modern Italy.* Princeton: Princeton University Press.

Pye, Lucian. 1966. *Aspects Of Political Development; An Analytic Study.* Boston: Little, Brown.

Rostow, W. W. 1960. *The Stages of Economic Growth.* Cambridge: Cambridge University Press.

Seligson, Mitchell and John Passé-Smith. 1998. *Development and Underdevelopment.* Boulder: Lynne Rienner.

Wallerstein, Immanuel. 1974. *The Modern World-System.* New York: Academic Press.

XIV
INTERNATIONAL
ORGANIZATIONS

In an attempt to maintain world order, nations have agreed to establish a series of formal institutions in the form of international organizations. These organizations are sites of international governance—while they do not govern state conduct directly, they provide a forum for the creation of agreements and norms on international conduct. The most important international organization is the United Nations.

The UN is a formal international organization with universal membership founded in 1945. The UN's founders designed it to work as a public forum for the whole world, and yet it operates under the constraints of its sovereign member states. Particularly today, the UN has a mandate to set the global agenda on a truly global range of issues, from food and shelter to nuclear energy and international finance. The effectiveness of UN decision-making and functional bodies, however, depends heavily on their perceived legitimacy.

There are several different ways to look at the UN, with each perspective revealing different aspects of its role and function (Luard and Heater, 1994). The UN can be seen as a set of decision-making components and functional units to implement the decisions. In this respect, the UN is an amalgam of familiar councils and commissions. Alternatively, the UN could be viewed as a group that operates according to the UN Charter. In this respect, it is the embodiment of international law. Some see the UN as an international bureaucracy, international civil servants independently serving the global interests. Many continue to view the UN as a collection of sovereign states. This collection reflects the will and interests of its members. The UN is all these things at once. It is an organization with two major purposes, as set forth in the preamble to the charter: Peace and Security, and Social Development. They are mutually reinforcing but afforded different weight by the different parts of the organization.

HISTORY AND DEVELOPMENT

The shape and function of the UN—specifically state representation and the Council system—reflect key trends in twentieth century history (Bennett, 1991). This brief historical overview highlights the key trends to which the founders of the UN were responding. Understanding the present state of the UN is possible only with an appreciation of the UN's original purpose in redressing these historical failures and capitalizing on historical opportunities.

World War I happened, in part, because there was no forum for international diplomacy. The great powers had no place to work out their differences and avoid war. Instead, they stumbled into a bloody and violent conflict. After the war, one of the items proposed in the Treaty of Versailles was the League of Nations. The League was in many ways a precursor to the UN, similar in many ways. It was intended to be a global body where nations could meet to settle their differences through diplomacy before resorting to war. It was designed to punish aggression and outlaw war. But, the League had several problems inherent in its design. First, not all states were members. Specifically, the defeated Germany was not allowed membership and the United

States refused to join. Therefore, the League did not contain two of the most powerful nations at the time. Additionally, the League operated on the rule of consensus, which in reality, meant that everyone had a veto. Since all League members had to agree to a decision, any one state could disagree and cause a stalemate. Thus, the League could not respond to the Japanese invasion of Manchuria in 1931 and the Italian invasion of Ethiopia in 1935 because the Italians and the Japanese blocked any decision that would have harmed themselves. The League could do nothing as international peace and security disappeared in the late 1930's. The onset of World War II represented the complete failure of the League of Nations as an international organization.

Toward the end of World War II, allied planners began to formulate plans for the post-war world order. They wanted to avoid the mistakes of the post World War I settlement and create a set of robust institutions that could avoid future global wars. The allied powers took the lead in the establishment of an international organization to avert further conflict through the maintenance of international peace and security and the promotion of social development.

The structure of the UN that exists today reflects the allies' attempts to deal with the conflicts of those times. The UN was given multiple organs to deal with the multiple items it was tasked with addressing. To avoid the problem of consensus that plagued the League, the committee of the whole, the General Assembly, was given only limited power. They realized that social development was a critical function for the new organization and created a set of organs to address social issues. The founders of the UN appreciated the fact that the great

powers of the time mattered more in the conduct of diplomacy
and the maintenance of peace and security than other states.
Without the cooperation of these great powers, the UN would
be deadlocked like the League and consigned to irrelevance. The
UN was established by the victorious powers of World War II:
the USA, the USSR, and the UK. France, as a liberated ally and
former great power, became a core ally. US President Roosevelt
wanted a state in Asia to counterbalance Russia and wanted to
promote China, a key ally against the Japanese. The founders of
the UN created the Security Council as a way to solve the
problems of the League. It would avoid the problems of
consensus, but appreciate the role of the five victorious great
powers. They knew that no issue of peace and security could be
resolved if a great power wanted to block it, and they knew that
they needed the cooperation of the great powers to make things
work. These nations became the permanent five on the UN
Security Council.

THE ORGANS OF THE UN

To meet its two major goals of the maintenance of peace and
security and social development, the UN has six major organs.
The centerpiece of the UN system is the General Assembly. All
UN members have a seat in the General Assembly; it is the only
forum where all the nations of the world meet in one place. It is
a plenary body for the purpose of expressing international
consensus on issues, and as a forum for debate and discussion of
international issues. The main function of the General Assembly
is as a forum for debate. The Assembly also oversees UN
administration, nominating members for other organs and
committees as well as setting the UN dues and budget. While
the General Assembly is a universal forum, which gives it

legitimacy, the General Assembly has few formal powers. General Assembly resolutions that deal with issues other than UN administration or admission of new members have questionable status as international law. The major committees of the General Assembly do produce resolutions that have led to international treaties. In essence, it deals more with image and discussion than power and enforcement.

The Security Council is the most powerful organ of the UN. The UN charter specifically gives the Security Council the primary responsibility for the maintenance of international peace and security. The Security Council is the only UN organ that can pass resolutions that are clearly binding on members as international law. If the Security Council calls for an action, members are obligated to respond. It is also the forum in which the UN debates the use of force, and it can authorize military action by member states as well as peace-keeping operations overseen by the UN. The Council has also created international tribunals to judge war criminals. In addition, the Council has played a role in the administration of the UN in picking a new Secretary General and admitting new members.

The Security Council's unique structure is a product of its historical role as the arbiter of international conflicts. There are 15 members of the Council. Five are permanent members: the US, the UK, Russia, France, and China. These five have a disproportionately large share of power in running the Council and thus the UN. The remaining ten Council members serve rotating two-year terms, with five new members seated each year. The Council seeks to have geographic diversity in its non-permanent members, and seats on the Council are a coveted accomplishment in UN diplomacy. The power of the permanent five members extends beyond their staying power. They also have a veto, which means they can block any resolution they choose. No resolution can pass the Council if a permanent member votes against it. Any member, including the permanent members, can abstain from a resolution, but it must have nine affirmative votes to pass. This structure reflects the historical conditions of the UN's creation. The permanent five members are the victorious powers of World War II. The veto prevents a great power clash within the UN that could destroy its legitimacy (Vincent, 1991).

This arrangement is not without controversy, however. The permanent five members no longer represent the world's greatest powers. The US and China remain strong, but the UK and France are past the height of their global influence. Russia's military potential and nuclear capability make it a global power, but its economy is not similarly large. Today's global powers such as Germany, Japan, India, Brazil, South Africa, and Nigeria are all absent from the Council. There have been calls to expand the Council to include more members, to add more permanent members, and even to take away the veto. But, of course, any of these proposals have to make it through the current system in which any of the permanent five could veto it. It is unlikely that the present permanent five will assent to any proposal that dilutes their current power position.

The Secretariat is led by the Secretary General and consists of several thousand international civil servants. These international bureaucrats administrate the daily business of the UN, translating conversations among delegates, making copies, and implementing policy decisions. The Secretary General is the public face of the UN, the individual charged with representing the body on the global stage. He is the only individual capable of speaking on behalf of the entire organization, and plays a critical role in global diplomacy. Yet the Secretary General faces a critical tension in his job. He is an extension of the will of the member states, doing what they direct. His role is to run the organization and implement the policies that the members approve. If he upsets the will of the member states, they can oust him from his position. At the same time, the Secretary General has an independent role to bring issues to the UN as he sees fit. He can intervene diplomatically in crises and can serve as a mediator in international conflicts. The Un Charter gives him both roles, and the managing of this tension is a key job of the Secretary General.

The International Court of Justice is the judicial organ of the UN system. This means that when member states have a dispute under international law, they can take each other to the ICJ, based in the Hague, the Netherlands. The 15 judges from all over the world hear and rule on the case. According to the UN charter, the decision of the ICJ is final and binding. But, the UN Charter also says that if the loser of a case does not comply with the ICJ ruling, the winner can take the issue to the Security Council. The ICJ has no enforcement mechanism of its own; it must rely on the Security Council to impose its will. However, if the loser of an ICJ case is one of the permanent five, it can veto any action against it. The great powers thus have a way out from complying with ICJ decisions. For example, in 1985 Nicaragua sued the US in the ICJ for illegally mining Nicaragua's harbors. While Nicaragua won the case, the US refused to comply with the ruling. Any appeals to the Security Council were blocked by the US's veto.

The Economic and Social Council, ECOSOC, is the organ that fulfills the second part of its mandate, social development. ECOSOC sponsors international discussions and research on issues of development. For example, it has created regional economic commissions which do research and have conferences to create new knowledge about economic development. Over the past 20 years, ECOSOC's influence as waned, but it still oversees a wide array of international development and social programs and committees.

The final organ of the UN is the Trusteeship Council. It was originally intended to facilitate the transition to independence of territories that had been European colonies. In 1994, Namibia was the last colony to gain independence. With no more colonies, the Trusteeship Council has no further business. There are proposals for developing a new mission for the Trusteeship Council, including assistance to failed states, like Somalia, or as a trustee for the global environment. This organ, however, remains defunct today.

OTHER ORGANIZATIONS

The UN is not the only major international organization—indeed, it is the center of a large family of organizations covering a wide variety of topics and functions. The UN family includes a number of UN specific organizations designed to implement UN programs and provide UN assistance to those in need. The UN Children's Fund (UNICEF), UN Development Program (UNDP), UN High Commission for Refugees (UNHCR), the World Food Program (WFP), the UN Education, Scientific, and Cultural Organization (UNESCO), and the UN Program on HIV/AIDS (AIDS), all better known by their acronym names, are just a small sampling of the myriad of organizations that the UN has created to implement particular programs and meet particular mandates.

Moreover, many international organizations not created by the UN are also part of the UN family. The International Atomic Energy Commission (IAEA), was created to implement the terms of the Nuclear Nonproliferation Treaty (NPT). The World Trade Organization (WTO) supervises a number of global trade agreements. The International Monetary Fund (IMF) and various members of the World Bank group are the international lenders created by the Bretton Woods Agreements. The International Labor Organization (ILO) and International Telecommunication Union (ITU) actually predate the founding of the UN. All of these organizations though are part of the larger UN family of international organizations that attempt to bring world order to international politics.

THE UN AT WORK

The UN faces both chronic and acute problems in international affairs, both of which it must deal with on an ongoing basis. Chronic international problems persist over time and affect a wide range of countries (Taylor and Groom, 1989). The UN addresses chronic problems through the GA and its committees to generate knowledge, awareness, and legitimacy. These committees have produced some important treaties. For instance, the Nuclear Non-Proliferation Treaty came out of the General Assembly committee on arms control. Because the UN is tasked with both maintaining peace and security and promoting growth and development, these issues compete for resources in the short term while ultimately reinforcing each other in the long run. The chronic problem of reinforcing peace and development is one of the UN's greatest challenges.

The UN also faces acute crises that rapidly flare up in specific locations. To address these acute crises, both the Security Council and Secretariat play an essential role. The Secretariat can deploy the UN's functional agencies such as UNHCR, UNHCHR and UNICEF to deliver immediate aid to states and people in trouble. The Security Council can either authorize individual member states to take action, or it can call for the deployment of peacekeeping troops under UN auspices. Peacekeeping was originally invented as a way for the UN to help monitor cease-fire agreements (Durch, 1993). Neutral troops, under UN authority, were sent to stand between warring factions to bolster the confidence that the other would follow the agreement. Since then, peacekeepers have taken on ever increasing roles, including stopping conflicts, protecting humanitarian aid, and rebuilding war-torn societies (Weiss, 1995).

TENSIONS IN THE UN

While it is a formal international organization officially supported by all its members who have agreed to its charter, the UN nevertheless faces a series of ongoing tensions. The first is that the UN can call on its member states to do things, but it has a hard time enforcing its own resolutions. It requires member states to contribute to peacekeeping operations and relief missions that the UN authorizes, but unless a state wants to contribute, it is an impotent body. The UN is continually faced with the tension between its role as an autonomous actor and collection of states. On the one hand, it can be argued that the values behind the UN Charter are universal and should apply to all. The UN has a mandate to work on its own to promote those values. On the other hand, the UN Charter is a treaty among states. Thus, the UN cannot do anything without the expressed approval of its members. The UN's authority comes from the states who join the organization, signed the charter, and provide the UN with the resources it needs to accomplish its mission.

The UN also faces the tension of the gap between the developed and developing world. The developing world represents the majority of the UN's members, both in terms of number of states and global population. The developed world controls the majority of resources available to the UN. Developing countries want the chance to build their societies, but much of this cannot be done without resources from the richer, already developed states who are reluctant to spend their resources on others. The struggle for resources and priorities is a constant tension within the UN.

Finally, there is a constant tension between the International Law of the UN Charter and the diplomacy that the member states conduct on a daily basis. The UN Charter has value only to the extent that states follow its provisions. States can ignore elements of the charter and can also work outside the Charter. Peacekeeping, for example, is never mentioned in the Charter but has become a key UN diplomatic function. Trying to maintain the integrity of international law while still playing effective diplomacy that satisfies the needs of the member states consumes much of the day-to-day business of the UN.

CONCLUSION

These tensions are manifest in the UN and what it does. The UN is a special international organization that reflects the historical conditions that produced it. It was designed to avoid a third world war and promote international peace and security as well as human social development. In many ways it has succeeded in these tasks, but it still has much more to accomplish.

BIBLIOGRAPHY

Bennett, A. LeRoy. 1991. *International Organizations: Principles and Issues*, 5th edition. Englewood Cliffs: Prentice Hall.

Durch, William. 1993. *The Evolution of UN Peacekeeping*. New York: St. Martins.

Luard, Evan and Derek Heater. 1994. *The United Nations: How it Works and What it Does*. New York: St. Martins.

Taylor, Paul and A. J. R. Groom. 1989. *Global Issues in the United Nations Framework*. New York: St. Martins.

Vincent, Jack. 1991. *Support Patterns at the United Nations*. Lanham: University Press of America.

Weiss, Thomas. 1995. *The United Nations and Civil Wars*. Boulder: Lynne Rienner.

XV
GLOBALIZATION

Globalization has something to do with the thesis that we now all live in one world—but in what way and how does globalization make the world a different place than 30, 20, or 10 years ago? Globalization has been influenced by technological innovations and developments in systems of communication, dating back only to the late 1960's. For example, in 1950 a three-minute telephone call from New York to London cost 50 dollars. In 1998, the cost of the same phone call cost 36 cents. While it took 40 years for radio in the United States to gain an audience of 50 million, it took only 15 years for computers to get 50 million users and 4 years for the internet to gain 50 million users. Globalization is used so often to describe our contemporary context that Zygmunt Bauman (1998) asserts that globalization is a fad word fast turning into a shibboleth, a magic incantation, a pass-key meant to unlock the gates to all present and future mysteries.

Numerous neologisms attempt to define the term: 'fragmegration' (Rossenau, 1996), 'globulation' (Friedman, 2000), and 'glocalization' (Svensson, 1991). Held et al (1999) identify three different schools of thought engaged in the globalization debate: hyperglobalizers, skeptics, and transformationalists. Hyperglobalizers argue that contemporary globalization defines a new era in which people's lives are increasingly subjected to the disciplines of the global market. The skeptical school argues that globalization is essentially a myth which conceals the reality of an international economy that is divided into three major regions: North America, Japan, and Europe. For the transformationalist camp, patterns of globalization are conceived as historically unprecedented so that states and societies across the globe are experiencing a process of profound change. Globalization is not only an economic or technological phenomenon but a political and cultural one as well.

DEFINING GLOBALIZATION

Globalization has many aspects, all tied to the notion that the world is shrinking. Some scholars used the concept of convergence to explain globalization. They argue that what we are witnessing in the world is a breakdown of barriers. News agency corporations such as CNN and the BBC have an audience that spans the global. As a result, much of the world's populations obtain their news from the same source. Fashion clothing, considered everyday wear in the "western world," is worn by individuals all over the world. This includes countries traditionally considered outside the "western world". The use of English as the official language for international interactions is increasing. Transnational business organizations such as Coca-cola and McDonald's are features of everyday life in many parts of the world, from Moscow to Dakar. The prevalence of Coca-Cola and McDonald's has been interpreted as a sign of American cultural and economic dominance, so that the world is becoming, or wanting to become, more like the United States. Contradicting the scholars mentioned above, others point out that convergence is coupled with divergence. As much as the world is becoming similar, there are also very clear differences. For example, McDonald's in India serves vegetarian hamburgers. These scholars argue against the notion that globalization equals Americanization or Westernization.

Others understand globalization as the compression of time and space (Harvey, 1989). They point out that distant events now have a significant impact on local affairs almost simultaneously. For instance, the Lovebug is a computer virus, created by a Filipino computer school student in the Philippines in 2000. The Lovebug virus destroyed computer files, stole passwords and e-mail addresses and replicated itself. Shortly after the virus was unleashed in cyberspace, it was estimated that the virus caused millions of dollars worth of damage to companies and organizations all around the world. Money, goods, people, and computer viruses are moving faster from one part of the world to another. In this chapter, globalization is defined as a process whereby political, economic, and socio-cultural transactions are less constrained by national boundaries and the sovereign authority of national governments.

THE HYPERGLOBALIZERS

For Kenichi Ohmae (1990), Richard O'Brien (2000) and Friedman (2000), globalization refers to increasing interconnections in the world and growing economic interdependence. More than a trillion dollars is turned over each day on global currency markets, a massive increase from only 10 years ago. The value of money we have in our pockets and bank accounts changes in accordance with fluctuations in global currency markets. One of the most significant features of a globalized world, as conceived by the hyperglobalizers, is the high level of finance and capital flows of electronic money—money that exists only as digits in computers. In the new global electronic economy, fund managers, banks, corporations, as well as millions of individual investors, can transfer vast amounts of capital from one side of the world to another at the click of a mouse. The global marketplace is much more complex than even two or three decades ago and is frequently indifferent to national borders. Governments cannot intervene in the economic and social life of their citizens in the same manner as before.

Although it creates winners and losers, nearly all countries have a comparative advantage in producing certain goods, which are then marketed in the global economy. Moreover, traditional nation-states have become unnatural/impossible business units in a global economy (Ohmae, 1990). The impulse of globalization is so strong that there are no alternative paths. Friedman likens globalization to dawn: if we were to try to stop it, human development would pay a huge cost. Globalization encapsulates a powerful thrust toward the realization of a market utopia on a world scale, with the opening of national economies, liberalization, and privatization. Although Ohmae and O'Brien agree on the decline of the importance of national economics, O'Brien's "end of geography" thesis stipulates that states are the source of current and future barriers. Despite these differences, for O'Brien and Ohmae, the rise of the global economy and the emergence of institutions of global governance and hybridization of cultures are evidence of a radically new world order—and they mean the demise of the prominence of the state. Over 1,500 *maquiladoras* (Spanish for US owned and operated assembly factories in Mexico) are located along the 2,100-mile border with the United States. These factories are not subject to Mexican labor laws. Although they provide jobs, they have been accused of offering poor health benefits and providing poor working conditions.

This perspective on globalization is somewhat problematic. First, globalization is conceived in a teleological manner. Given time, developing countries will catch up with the North America and Western Europe. Technology is presented as the driving force of social change. Given that no one predicted that the processes of globalization would take place, it is problematic to predict how globalization will proceed. This view presents globalization as a benign process. However, there is the growing gap between the rich and the poor within countries and between states. The share of the poorest fifth of the world's population in global income has dropped from 2.3% to 1.4% over the past 10 years. The proportion taken by the richest fifth, on the other hand, has risen from 70% to 85%. More critically though, what is missing in this account is the notion of the historically and socially embedded conditions within which globalization is taking place. For example, UNDP report states that Americans spend more than $8 billion a year on cosmetics—$2 billion more than the estimated annual total needed to provide basic education for everyone in the world. In 1996 alone Ethiopia had a total foreign debt of $10 billion, whilst in the same year Europe spent $11 billion on ice cream. The three richest people in the world have assets that exceed the combined gross domestic product of the 48 least developed countries. This viewpoint on globalization emphasizes the geographical aspects and de-emphasizes the historical context of the phenomenon.

THE SKEPTICAL SCHOOL

Skeptics of globalization argue that it is not a new phenomenon. Whatever patterns we see happening in the world, have happened before. Whatever globalization's benefits, trials and tribulations, the level of global transactions is not especially different from other periods in history. In the late nineteenth Century, there was already an open global economy, with plenty of trade including trade in currencies. During the Trans-Atlantic African slave trade, millions of people were bought and sold in markets all over the world. Skeptics also point out that Transnational Corporations are not new organizations, citing the existence of the Dutch East India Company, which was a conglomeration of several small, independent trading companies in the 1600s in the Netherlands. The main purpose of the company was to promote trade with Asia. What is significant is that the new company was given extensive powers by the government of the Netherlands to help it achieve better trade with Asia. These powers included the rights to enter into treaties, to maintain military forces and powers of government and justice. Powers that traditionally belong to states were given to the Dutch East India company; similarly, many transnational corporations enjoy these powers today.

For scholars such as Hirst and Thompson (1996) and Boyer and Drache (1996), globalization as conceived by extreme "globalizers" is a myth. Contemporary levels of economic interdependence are not historically unprecedented. What is called globalization today is less significant than the regime that prevailed from 1870 to 1914. Hirst and Thompson offer two models of the world economy: an international economy and a global economy. They argue that instead of globalization what we have is internationalization. In an international economy, the principal entities are national economies. As evidence of the centrality of national economies, Hirst and Thompson point to the fact that Japanese companies are reluctant to locate core functions such as research and development abroad. Skeptics criticize underestimating the enduring power of national governments. Linda Weiss (1997) argues that the "state denial" argument is blind to the variety of state responses to international pressures. What we should focus on is the "transformative capacity" of states—the ability to adapt to external shocks and pressures by generating new means of governing the processes of industrial change.

In the same vein, Leo Panitch (1996) states that capitalist globalization is a process which takes place, in, through, and under the aegis of the state. It is encoded by them, and in many respects it is authored by them. During the 1990's, President Clinton and his advisers, including Robert Rubin, Lawrence Summers, and Stanley Fisher set out on a mission to implement the free-market system to developing countries. Joseph Stiglitz, Clinton's chief economic adviser at the time and then chief economist at the World Bank, argues in his new book Globalization and its Discontents (2001) that globalization designed by top officials of the United States government became a neo-imperialist force that left hundreds of millions of people worse off in 2000 than they were in 1990. In Sub-Saharan Africa, 20 countries have lower incomes per head in real terms than they did two decades ago. He argues that the Treasury Department and the IMF, which follows the preferences of Washington, DC, its largest shareholder, used huge loans to compel governments to follow economic policies that did not address the specific problems of many countries. Free trade produced another set of social and economic problems in some countries. Opening up a country or regions within it to free trade can undermine a local subsistence economy. An area that becomes dependent upon a few products sold on world markets is very vulnerable to shifts in prices. In some cases, stringent economic reforms resulted in a loss of state resources to help the poor. In parts of the former Soviet Union, there has been an increase in the number of poor children. More than 40 percent of Eastern Europe's populations live in poverty.

According to the skeptical school, internationalization has not been accompanied by decreased global inequalities. Capital mobility is not producing a shift of investment and employment from advanced to developing countries. In essence, then the world economy is not 'global'—rather, trade, investment, and financial flows are concentrated in the triad of Europe, Japan, and North America. Like hyperglobalizers, skeptics come from an overly economic perspective and ascribe a teleological nature to globalization. This notion of globalization implies that the path that globalization has tread in advanced capitalist countries will be mirrored in other countries of the world. The present is seen as a stepping stone in some linear progression. Furthermore, factors that cannot be empirically measured such as cultural change do not enter into the framework described above. Skeptics argue that there is nothing new under the sun. However, this view points to the continuities in the world economy while silent about the discontinuities. This approach is silent about change and offers no way for us to recognize change when it takes place.

THE TRANSFORMATION THESIS

From this perspective, processes of globalization are historically unprecedented such that governments and societies across the globe have to adjust to a world in which there is no longer a clear distinction between international and domestic affairs. Globalization is a contingent historical process replete with contradictions. It integrates as it fragments (Rosennau, 1996). Traditional views of North/South distinctions are rendered impotent—they are no longer geographic but social. These distinctions are no longer out there, but nestled together within all the world's major cities. How do scholars in this camp define globalization? According to this school of thought, globalization is not a single unified phenomenon. As Mittelman (2000) puts it is a 'syndrome' of processes and activities. Integral to the syndrome are the interactions among the global division of labor and power, the new regionalism, and resistance politics. So, the dominant form of globalization means a historical transformation: in the economy; in livelihoods and modes of existence; in politics.

For Held et al (1999) globalization refers to the widening, deepening and speeding-up of global interconnectedness. This growing extensity, intensity, and velocity of global interactions may be associated with a deepening enmeshment of the local and global such that the impact of distant events is magnified and the most local developments may come to have global consequences. Held et al, however, map the shape and consequences of globalization by focusing on states in advanced capitalist societies (SIACS). This begs the question: what is new then?

For Giddens (1991) and Harvey (1989) globalization is not only new, but also revolutionary; it is the compression of time and space. Space is distinct from place (a physical setting) as it has a social dimension to it. This process not only pulls upwards, but also pushes downwards, creating new pressures for local autonomy. It also squeezes sideways, creating new economic and cultural zones within and across nations. These definitions exclude power asymmetries and silence the conflicts and power relations. However, only certain people form territorial constraints while denuding the territory to which other people go on being confined. Bauman (1998) stresses the importance of nomadic capital. As he puts it, the new freedom of capital is reminiscent of that of the "absentee landlords" of yore, notorious for their neglect of the needs of the working populations. In contradistinction to the absentee landlords of early modern times, the late-modern capitalists, because of electronic capital flows, do not always face the wrath of the populations. They have little difficulty packing their tents and finding more hospitable environments.

Who/what drives globalization? Giddens (2000) states that globalization is becoming increasingly de-centered—not under the control of any group of nations. He refers to "reverse colonization" by which he means that non-Western countries influence developments in the West. Examples include the Latinizing of Los Angeles, the emergence of a globally oriented high-tech sector in India, or the selling of Brazilian television programs to Portugal. Although nobody is totally in control, Giddens states that globalization has been influenced above all by developments in systems of communication, dating back only to the late 1960s. As mentioned above, it took 40 years for radio in the US to gain an audience of 50 million. The same number was had adapted the personal computers in 15 years. In a mere 4 years, 40 million Americans were regularly using the Internet. For Castells (2000) it is the information technology revolution and the restructuring of capitalism that drive globalization. As a result we have a new society, the "network society". The network society is characterized by the globalization of strategically decisive economic activities.

CONCLUSION

Unlike the scholars in the hyperglobalizers' camp, the transformation school does not declare the end of the state. Nor do they give primacy to the strength of the state (like some skeptics claim). In fact Giddens refers to "shell institutions" (nation, family, etc)—the outer shell remains, but inside they have changed.

BIBLIOGRAPHY

Bauman, Zygmunt. 1998. *Globalization: The Human Consequences.* New York: Columbia University Press.

Boyer and Drache. 1996. *States Against Markets: The Limits Of Globalization.* New York: Routledge.

Castells, Manuel. 2000. *The Rise Of The Network Society.* Cambridge: Blackwell Publishers.

Giddens, Anthony. 1991. *Modernity And Self-Identity: Self And Society In The Late Modern Age.* Stanford: Stanford University Press.

Giddens. Anthony. 2000. *How Globalization is Reshaping Our Lives* New York: Routledge.

Harvey, David. 1989. *The Condition of Postmodernity.* Cambridge: Blackwell Publishers.

Held, David, et al. 1999. *Global Transformations: Politics, Economics and Culture.* Stanford: Stanford University Press.

O'Brien, Richard. 1992. *Global Financial Integration: The End of Geography.* New York: Council on Foreign Relations Press.

Ohmae, Kenichi. 1985. *Triad Power: The Coming Shape of Global Competition.* New York: Free Press.

Stiglitz, Joseph. 2002. *Globalization and its Discontents.* New York: W.W. Norton.

Weiss, Linda. 1998. *The Myth of The Powerless State.* Ithaca: Cornell University Press.

INDEX

About the Author

Dr. Mehdi Heravi, Professor, University Administrator, Editor, is author of a number of books and articles. Dr. Heravi is listed in *American Men of Social and Behavioral Sciences, Who's Who in America*, and *Who's Who in the World*. He also received Scroll of Legend from Cambridge, and in 2004 by the authority of the United Cultural Convention he was awarded its International Peace prize.